Personality Disorders - New Findings and Treatments

Edited by María-José Martín-Vázquez

Published in London, United Kingdom

Personality Disorders - New Findings and Treatments
http://dx.doi.org/10.5772/intechopen.1009069
Edited by María-José Martín-Vázquez

Contributors
Akanksha Shankar, Ayse Dondu, Estefanía Pinzón-Kranz, Hafiz Shafique Ahmad, Jesús Vaca-Cortés, Joel Monárrez-Espino, Khizra Mussadiq, Lorena Ávila-Carrasco, Luisa Villareal-Varela, Margarita Martínez-Fierro, María-José Martín-Vázquez, Shubham Sharma

First published in London, United Kingdom, 2025 by IntechOpen
IntechOpen is the global imprint of INTECHOPEN LIMITED, registered in England and Wales, registration number: 11086078, 167-169 Great Portland Street, London, W1W 5PF, United Kingdom

For EU product safety concerns: IN TECH d.o.o., Prolaz Marije Krucifikse Kozulić 3, 51000 Rijeka, Croatia, info@intechopen.com or visit our website at intechopen.com.

British Library Cataloguing-in-Publication Data
A catalogue record for this book is available from the British Library

Personality Disorders - New Findings and Treatments
Edited by María-José Martín-Vázquez
p. cm.

This title is part of the Nervous System and Mental Health Book Series, Volume 4
Series Editor: Toshikazu Shinba

Print ISBN 978-0-85466-176-3
Online ISBN 978-0-85466-175-6
eBook (PDF) ISBN 978-0-85466-177-0
ISSN 3050-2985

If disposing of this product, please recycle the paper responsibly.

IntechOpen Book Series

Nervous System and Mental Health

Volume 4

Aims and Scope of the Series

Mental health is frequently linked to the nervous system. Conversely, disturbances in the nervous system often lead to mental health problems. However, this linkage is not as clear as it is commonly accepted. Mental health is usually described using subjective terms, which are based on psychological and psychiatric symptomatology. Diagnosis of a mental illness is made through the presence of the subjective symptoms characterizing the illness.

On the other hand, the nervous system has been deeply investigated using objective measures, including molecular, genetic, imaging, pharmacological and physiological ones. It is essential to combine objective views of the nervous system with subjective perspectives on mental health to develop an integrative approach to understanding human cognitive functions and achieving overall well-being. In this book series, experts in various fields of the nervous system and mental health will present their views on these challenging topics.

Meet the Series Editor

Dr. Toshikazu Shinba is a psychiatrist and neuroscientist who has been working in both clinical and basic research fields. He has been affiliated with the Tokyo Institute of Psychiatry, Department of Neurophysiology and Stress Disorders Project, and now works as a psychiatrist at Shizuoka Saiseikai General Hospital, Department of Psychiatry. The primary focus of his research is the electrophysiological analysis of attention and arousal in both humans and rodents. In clinical research, EEG, heart rate variability and skin conductance have been measured in mental disorders and arousal/consciousness disturbances. In basic research, single neuronal firing and EEG recordings have been assessed in rats. His research interests cover physiological rhythms related to attention, arousal, and consciousness in both the central and peripheral nervous systems, with a focus on understanding mental states.

Meet the Volume Editor

María-José Martín-Vázquez is a psychiatrist and psychologist, with a doctorate in Medicine from Alcalá de Henares University, and a Professor of Psychiatry at Universidad Europea de Madrid. She has been working as the person responsible for the severe personality disorder program in the area of San Sebastián de los Reyes / Alcobendas, in Madrid (Spain). She has published more than 80 articles and book chapters, and she is the editor of a book, "Manual of use of psychotropic medication in medical illness". She serves as a reviewer for several international publishers. Finally, she has a background in psychodynamics, psychology, bioethics, and law, as well as experience in EMDR, transference-focused psychotherapy, and effective psychiatric management. Her doctoral thesis is a work about bipolar disorder and voice changes. Currently, she is a member of the Assistential Ethics Committee at Hospital Infanta Sofía in Madrid.

Contents

Preface

The management of personality disorders has experienced an important change in the last decades, with an increased interest in the study of these disorders. Personality disorders are highly prevalent, overall, in clinical settings. Until the end of the twentieth century, the treatment of personality disorders was considered almost impossible, and a diagnosis of personality disorders was a confirmation of intractability and bad prognosis.

Over the last thirty years, research on personality disorders has grown exponentially due to the development of efficient psychotherapeutic strategies. In this book, authors from around the world have shared their knowledge with readers.

Firstly, the book offers new insights into the neurobiology of personality disorders, an exciting field of research that provides a different perspective on personality traits. Also, this chapter reviews the various systems of classification of this pathology.

The second chapter of the first section is dedicated to a study on the motivation behind criminal behavior in adolescents, which may help explain the antisocial traits that often persist into adulthood. This is particularly relevant since antisocial personality disorder is frequently forgotten in the psychiatric literature, and any data about its origin could help to understand the possible prevention and treatment.

We continue with a panoramic view of the latest findings in personality research and treatment, as well as psychiatric and psychotherapeutic interventions available for managing these disorders.

The second section is dedicated to the treatment of personality disorders. The fourth chapter reviews evidence-based strategies in psychotherapy for personality disorders, with a focus on the four main approaches: dialectical behavior therapy, transference-focused psychotherapy, mentalization-based psychotherapy, and general psychiatric management. It also includes a section about the use of EMDR in these patients.

And finally, the book closes with an interesting chapter about schema therapy, a strategy that has demonstrated its utility for depression, and it is being used for the treatment of depressive symptoms in personality disorders, with promising results.

The editor, the authors, and all the editorial staff are proud of the work that was done and are now seeing daylight. We hope that this book will meet the expectations of readers and contribute to the knowledge, understanding, and treatment of an exciting and, at times, overlooked field of study, such as personality disorders. We would like to share this book with all the mental health professionals.

María-José Martín-Vázquez, MD PhD
Department of Psychiatry and Mental Health,
Infanta Sofía University Hospital,
FIIB HUIS-HUHEN,
Spain

Faculty of Medicine, Health and Sports,
Department of Medicine,
European University of Madrid,
Madrid, Spain

Section 1

New Findings in Personality Disorders

Chapter 1

Emerging Insights in the Neurobiology and Classification of Personality Disorders

Hafiz Shafique Ahmad and Khizra Mussadiq

Abstract

This document explains the neurological bases of personality disorders, mainly giving special attention to Borderline and Antisocial Personality Disorders. By putting together structural, functional, molecular, and genetic-epigenetic elements, it points out the many aspects involved in personality pathology. It rejects the use of single labels for diagnosing people, urging the use of models that are backed by scientific research on the brain and chemicals. Talking about neurobiology means covering special therapy plans, usually with medicines and emerging neuromodulation techniques. Special concerns about biomarkers, cultures, and brain development of children are discussed in this research. In short, the plan is to use a variety of methods and study connections among mental health factors to create better ways to diagnose and treat patients and increase outcomes for them.

Keywords: personality disorders, neurobiology, dimensional classifications, cognitive-behavioral therapy, dialectical behavioral therapy, pharmacologic trials

1. Introduction

Studying personality disorders with the help of neuroscientific tools and special imaging has led to significant changes in psychopathology. It used to be reasoned that personality disorders were interpreted mainly through watching people's actions and self-exploration. Still, presently, most studies see structural and functional brain anomalies as the core reason behind their development. Many professionals have pointed out that the exact boundaries and overlapping nature of the hard categories in the Diagnostic and Statistical Manual of Mental Disorders, 5th edition, text revision (DSM-5-TR) and International Classification of Diseases, 11th revision (ICD-11) tend to give more than one diagnosis and cause challenges in choosing the best way to treat a patient [1, 2]. Researchers now think that Borderline Personality Disorder (BPD) and Antisocial Personality Disorder (ASPD) occur along a range since painful and uncontrolled emotions and thoughts can affect nearly everyone to some degree. With this new way of looking at things, neuroimaging data are now considered essential for making choices in diagnostics and treatment.

It has now been agreed that personality disorders involve certain brain areas based on recent research. Using functional magnetic resonance imaging (fMRI) and positron emission tomography (PET) scans, various studies always point out that the amygdala, the insula, and the prefrontal cortex are abnormal in psychopaths. For example, people with BPD usually have overactive amygdala, which results in them easily feeling emotions and having challenges controlling negative feelings. As an alternative, people with ASPD are likely to have little activity in the amygdala and prefrontal cortex, which means less fear conditioning, poorer moral reasoning, and more often engaging in risks [3]. All these point to the idea that problems with neural mechanisms contribute to both instability in emotions and relationships in BPD as well as the cruel and unrestrained behavior in ASPD. In this way, insights like this help explain the basis of problems in someone's personality and also look for possible ways to identify and help in the early stages.

Apart from physical changes in the brain, neurobiology research is providing more information on the way personality disorders change and develop. Scientists have found links between a person's genes, adverse situations, and growing brain development, which together contribute to changes in brain structure. Having experienced such as abuse in childhood tends to weaken the brain structures that help control stress. Because of this, the normal development of the prefrontal cortex and amygdala is affected, which, in time, leads to the formation of maladaptive personality traits [4]. Furthermore, recent studies track the development of personality using neuroimaging tools, proving that this disorder affects people during the whole course of their lives. Because of developmental findings, we should aim for prevention by using models that include both biological and other risk factors, instead of waiting until the late stages to label someone.

All in all, new techniques have revealed how brain functions are involved in the difficulties and symptoms of personality disorders. Using brain images with other diagnostic tools may help improve the accuracy of care and shift the approach from only listing symptoms to methods based on brain science. Adjusting the view in this way agrees with a framework that covers a wide range of personality dysfunctions and supports the progress of future clinical and research work.

2. Historical background and theoretical foundations

Originally, personality disorders were understood through a framework influenced a lot by psychoanalysis and descriptions, paying little attention to brain or biological factors. Earlier, the Diagnostic and Statistical Manual of Mental Disorders (DSM) and similar systems mainly relied on what could be seen in a patient's actions and symptoms without paying attention to their biological factors [1]. Since they assumed that personality traits are always clear and sharp, they developed models to label pathological disorders, such as Borderline, Narcissistic, or Antisocial Personality Disorder. Yet, it did not take long for clinicians and researchers to spot the restrictions of this concept, such as many diagnoses being linked with other mental health issues and that most types of diagnoses change over time. A lot of the subjects fulfilled the requirements for more than one personality disorder, and some diagnoses even changed in different evaluations, proving that firm classifications are not real. Because of this lack of predictability, both treating patients and understanding personality pathology became harder, which made it necessary to look at the issue from a different point of view [1].

According to Paris [5], researchers using the traditional method to diagnose personality disorders would only describe the behaviors and failed to consider results from neuroscience and genetics. Using this procedure made it easier for doctors to communicate and analyze cases. Still, it did not answer the main questions relating to the beginnings and biological processes of the diseases. The lack of attention to brain biology in the field made it stand still, especially when compared to other parts of psychiatry that improved significantly due to neuroimaging and studies on molecules. Because of these redefinitions, disorders such as schizophrenia and major depressive disorder led to biological treatments being used. Unlike depression, thoughts about personality disorders continued to focus mainly on psychodynamic and behavioral theories, which do not say much about the development and genetics involved in lasting personality problems [5].

Since comorbidities and significant differences are found in the categorical model, researchers began to use ways that describe personality disorders along a spectrum instead. New information from neuroimaging experiments and molecular genetics became available and pointed to recognizable issues with brain functions that accompanied different personality traits. To gain insight into this, Schmaal et al. [6] looked at big brain imaging studies to find differences in emotion regulation, hindrance of impulsive behaviors, and social abilities that are common to personality disorders. The results proved that models describing continuums in human behavior are more supported by science since they better link brain changes with certain personality aspects than with diagnostic labels in DSM. Findings indicated that personality pathologies are biological in nature and can easily be measured in various people [6].

Also speaking in favor of the dimensional approach, Ruocco and Carcone [4] provided scientific evidence showing that personality disorders are best understood by using both psychological and biological perspectives. Their review showed regular changes in activity and connections in the brain's amygdala, anterior cingulate cortex (ACC), and prefrontal cortex in people with different personality disorders. These regions are needed for identifying risks, emotional control, and decision-making, all of which resemble the typical signs of personality disorders like feeling moody, having little power, and experiencing difficulties in relationships. It was suggested by the authors that the combination of brain scans and personality traits calls for changing how we classify personality disorders, as they represent extreme behaviors on essential personality traits affected by various factors in the brain and environment [4]. By using this approach, one can understand personality-related issues more fully by adding genes, brain development, and life experiences into the same explanation.

Influences from molecular biology, which resulted in finding connections between genes and personality, have contributed to the change from categorical to dimensional models of personality. Using genome-wide association studies (GWAS), specific gene mutations connected to the development of personality disorders have been found, mainly when these disorders are linked to serotonin and dopamine activity. Such findings indicate that personal traits are shaped by both biology and the environment, and some of them might become harmful to a person if certain conditions occur. When someone has a gene variation related to serotonin, they may be vulnerable to difficulty controlling emotions and impulse control, the usual features of Borderline Personality Disorder, if they go through early life trauma [6]. Using information from molecular studies, it is easier to understand the gene-to-brain-to-behavior pathways and identify specific places to treat each early and effectively.

In addition, the dimensional point of view matches up better with today's personality psychology, mainly the Five-Factor Model (FFM), which is widely used and has strong support from many cultures. The FFM claims that there are five core dimensions of personality—neuroticism, extraversion, openness to experience, agreeableness, and conscientiousness—and each of them runs from one extreme to the other. Many studies have revealed that personality disorders are seen as irregular forms of standard traits in people. As an example, when neuroticism is very high and agreeableness and conscientiousness are very low, it is closely connected to several personality disorders, such as BPD and ASPD [5]. Such models give researchers a simpler framework to understand personality disorders and also cover the different and complicated ways that people may display the disorders. It allows for treatments that fit the individual's needs and development better because it examines the whole range of personality behaviors, instead of using set limits for diagnosing.

One reason why neurobiological evidence was slow to be included in the study of personality disorders is that psychoanalytic and humanistic approaches focused on people's subjective experiences and the way they interact with others instead of biological factors. Though these views have helped to understand the lives of people with personality disorders, they generally disagreed with biological reasons and regarded them as too simplistic. Nevertheless, new results from both neuroscience and genetics are leading more people to accept that personality involves biology. Neurobiological studies go along with psychology, beefing up existing theories about how traits in personality start, remain present, and can change in harmful ways [4]. It sees personality as a result of the mix of genetic features, growth throughout life, and the influence of society; this way, it gives science and practice a better, whole approach.

As a result of these new trends, DSM-5's Section III now outlines the Alternative Model of Personality Disorders (AMPD) that use both approaches to criteria. It is a radical change from the previous system, as it mainly focuses on problems and traits in a person's personality to determine a diagnosis. Because it is based on modern studies in personality psychology and neuroscience, the model is more useful for clinicians. People have praised the AMPD for representing personality disorders in detail, separating various types of disorders, and supporting the dependability and accuracy of tests (2022). Furthermore, the AMPD assists by placing neurobiological findings into clinical practice by making diagnoses fit with traits that can be measured through behavior, brain scans, and genes. When clinical practice joins forces with empirical science, it becomes a significant advance in handling personality disorders.

According to the World Health Organization's ICD-11, instead of having various personality disorders, evaluations are based on how severe the symptoms are. Dichotomous classification looks at how well a person functions based on five negative traits: affectivity, detachment, dissociability, disinhibition, and anaplastic. The developers of ICD-11 made it more useful in clinical situations and applicable to various cultures while matching the latest research on the biological and emotional background of personality issues [2]. The move to use dimensional models in DSM-5 and ICD-11 marks the view shared by many experts that personality disorders involve many factors that cannot be easily sorted into categories. Therefore, adding information from neurobiology, developmental psychopathology, and personality science to diagnosing, research, and therapy is now more critical than before.

All things considered, how personality disorder has been diagnosed has displayed a broader shift in psychology, from simply thinking about symptoms to exploring the links between biology and psychology. Although traditional approaches helped clinicians, their shortcomings regarding the accuracy of diagnostics and discovering the causes of illnesses have resulted in reviewing their main ideas. Paris [5] points out that personality disorder research will move forward by uniting information from both descriptive and explanatory theories, plus what is discovered in neuroscience, molecular biology, and personality psychology. Based on Schmaal et al. [6] and Ruocco and Carcone [4], neurobiological findings seem to strengthen our knowledge and help us treat and diagnose personality disorders more accurately. To enhance efforts against personality disorders, we should improve and combine dimensional models with biological knowledge, which will result in a fairer, more effective, and science-based treatment for those who deal with these conditions (**Table 1**).

Key aspect	Description	Reference(s)
Early Diagnostic Approach	Initially based on psychoanalytic descriptions and observable behaviors, with little attention to biology or brain science.	American Psychiatric Association [1]
Limitations of Categorical Models	Diagnoses lacked consistency, often overlapped, and changed over time, reducing reliability and making treatment harder.	American Psychiatric Association [1]
Neglect of Biology	Traditional methods ignored neuroscience and genetics, limiting understanding of origins and mechanisms of disorders.	Paris [5]
Advancements in Neuroscience	Brain imaging revealed dysfunctions in emotion regulation, impulse control, and social behavior associated with various personality traits.	Schmaal et al. [6]
Neurobiological Insights	Brain regions like the amygdala and prefrontal cortex are implicated in personality traits and disorders, supporting integration of biology and psychology.	Ruocco & Carcone [4]
Genetic Findings	GWAS link gene variations (especially involving serotonin and dopamine) to disorders like BPD, suggesting interaction between genes and early trauma.	Schmaal et al. [6]
Support for Dimensional Models	Dimensional models better reflect biological data and variability in symptoms than fixed categories.	Ruocco & Carcone [4]; Paris [5]
Alignment with FFM	Dimensional diagnosis aligns with Five-Factor Model (neuroticism, extraversion, openness, agreeableness, conscientiousness) for a broader, trait-based understanding.	Paris [5]
Critique of Traditional Models	Psychoanalytic and humanistic views prioritized subjective experience, resisting biological simplifications.	Ruocco & Carcone [4]
Adoption of AMPD in DSM-5	Section III includes the Alternative Model for Personality Disorders, combining trait-based and functional criteria, backed by neuroscience and personality research.	American Psychiatric Association [1]
ICD-11 Dimensional Model	Classifies based on severity and five core traits: affectivity, detachment, dissociability, disinhibition, and anaplastic behavior. Designed for clinical utility across cultures.	World Health Organization [2]
Call for Integration	Emphasis on unifying biological, psychological, and developmental insights to enhance diagnosis, understanding, and treatment of personality disorders.	Paris [5]; Schmaal et al. [6]
Future Outlook	A shift toward models that integrate dimensionality with neurobiological evidence promises more personalized and effective care.	Ruocco & Carcone [4]; Paris [5]

Table 1.
Evolution from categorical to dimensional models in personality disorder diagnosis.

3. Neurobiological correlates of personality disorders

3.1 Structural and functional imaging findings

With the help of special magnetic resonance imaging (MRI) technology and structural and functional magnetic resonance imaging (fMRI), it is now possible to explore the mysterious area of personality disorders with reliable information. An important discovery in the study of BPD is that the prefrontal cortex and amygdala areas of the brain are usually dysregulated. The prefrontal cortex is less active during an fMRI brain scan in people with impulsive disorder, which affects areas like self-control, decision-making, and emotional reactions. By contrast, sometimes the amygdala reacts too strongly to things that may cause fear or anger, mainly in situations where it's not clear what the correct response should be. The happening of both patterns at the same time is why a person with BPD struggles with strong emotions and aggressive actions and becomes easily sensitive toward others [7, 8]. In addition, findings of abnormal communication between the amygdala and prefrontal cortex in BPD patients have been confirmed in several tests, proving they are a reliable marker **Figure 1**.

It has been observed in ASPD that there are problems with the way specific neural route's function. It has been found in such studies that the orbitofrontal cortex (OFC), which participates in understanding emotions, making moral decisions, and controlling one's actions, shows less activity in people with antisocial personality disorder. Such hypofunction might be the reason for the main traits of ASPD, such as being insensitive,

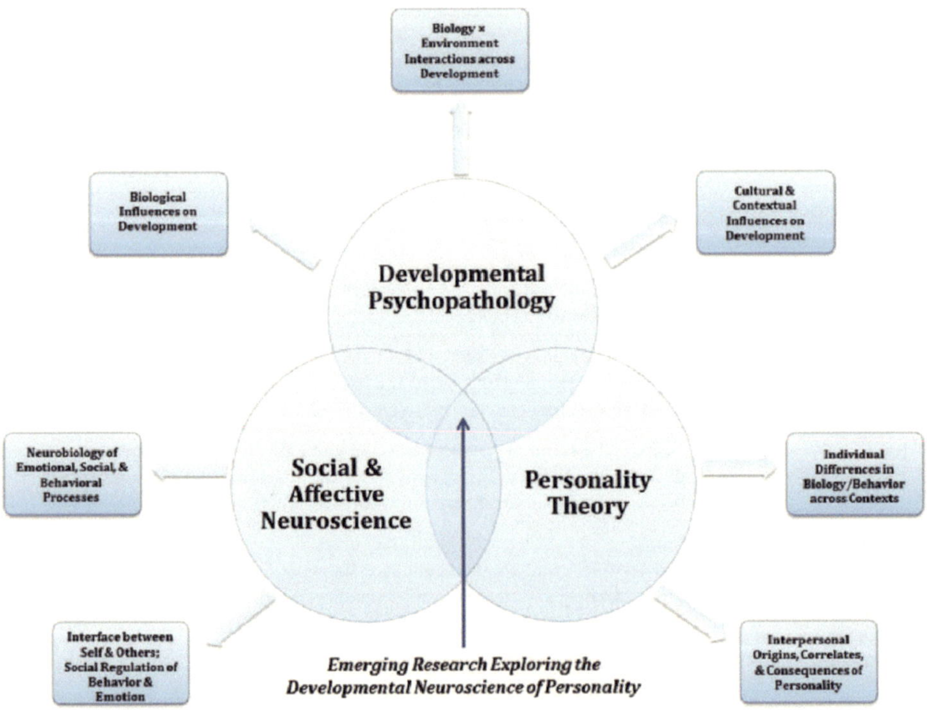

Figure 1.
Emerging research exploring the developmental neuroscience of personality. Source: Spytska [9].

ignoring social expectations, and lacking feelings of remorse. The researchers [3] found weaker OFC responses during tasks involving emotion and judgment about morality, confirming that ASPD causes the brain to work differently in moral functions. Besides, those with ASPD have issues with the ACC, which, together with the OFC, supports cognitive empathy and monitoring of errors, both needed for fitting into society.

New ways like graph theory analysis have helped explain the altered structure of the brain in these disorders. According to D'Adda et al. [10], greater corticolimbic alterations occurred in patients with BPD and ASPD, such as lowering global efficiency and changes in module forms. According to the research, changes in the brain linked to personality disorders can spread to many areas of the brain. This way of thinking shows that it may be essential to treat problems using methods that affect different brain systems rather than just one small structure. All in all, neuroimaging investigations make it evident that personality disorders have roots in brain structure as well as function.

3.2 Molecular and neurochemical insights

In addition to changes in the brain's structure and functions, unusual levels of chemicals in the brain cause personality disorders. Scientists have mainly focused on the neurotransmitter serotonin (5-HT) because of its role in regulating impulses, controlling aggression, and influencing moods. Decreased function of serotonin inside the prefrontal cortex and limbic system is the main neurochemical feature shared by BPD and ASPD. According to Coccaro et al. [11], the brain's serotonin levels are dysfunctional in cases of both conditions and impulsive aggression. It is suggested that these changes happen because the brain's serotonin pathways do not work as well, making it hard to stop behaving aggressively or impulsively. Consequently, several psychological problems can be managed with medications, although only selective serotonin reuptake inhibitors (SSRIs) might help with some personality illnesses.

There are now better details available about brain chemistry because of recent progress in PET imaging. Researchers like Davis et al. [12] saw that the quantity of metabotropic glutamate receptor subtype 5 (mGluR5) was lower in BPD patients who had a history of suicide attempts. Even though the glutamatergic system is not as well known as serotonin, it dramatically influences the plasticity of synapses and emotions. Based on these results, BPD's high suicide rate could be a result of unbalanced glutamate in the brain. Moreover, it seems that the mGluR5 receptor controls the neural systems associated with pleasure and emotional feelings, so reducing this receptor might bring about mood swings and impulsive actions found in BPD patients.

Another set of chemicals getting increasing attention for personality disorders is called oxytocin. It has been found that oxytocin, which contributes to making connections, trust, and empathy, is imbalanced in people with BPD. According to Herpetz and Bertsch [7], people with BPD have less noticeable oxytocin responses to situations of social stress. This was taken as an indicator that the issues these patients have with others could be connected to hormonal changes. The results support the use of social neuroscience theories to describe personality disorders since these issues mainly involve social and relationship challenges. So, studies of molecules and brain chemistry show that personality disorders are related to many alterations in the brain.

3.3 Genetic and epigenetic contributions

It is becoming evident that personality disorders are influenced by gene activity as well as its regulation, supported by various twin research, GWAS, and imaging studies. Half or more of the reasons for personality are related to biological influences, but personality also depends on environment and genetics [5]. They point out that genetics plays a significant role in explaining why certain people have personality disorders. By reviewing research papers on imaging genetics, Schmaal et al. [6] pointed out that different gene variants in the serotonin and dopamine systems are related to the observed brain changes in BPD. To be more specific, these variations are linked to changes in amygdala activity and a lowered activity in the prefrontal areas, as found in neuroimaging studies. Because of the link between genetics and neurobiology, it seems logical that neurotransmitter-based differences in genes play a significant role in forming the brain, often seen in personality disorders.

Besides the influence of genes, epigenetic processes are also vital in showing personality pathology. Epigenetics happens when some genes are affected by events before birth or in our lives, but the changes are not written in the DNA. They pointed out that how the environment and genes work together is key to learning about the different aspects of personality disorders. Because of this, methylation in genes that run the hypothalamic-pituitary-adrenal (HPA) axis can be affected by childhood maltreatment and change emotional and stress-related behaviors in adulthood. Evidence is beneficial for Borderline Personality Disorder because suffering from trauma is frequent and dramatically affects how bad the disorder is.

Epigenetic activities in the brain are known to be affected by heightened population density, constant changes in the environment, and strain on people's finances and work in cities. According to Khalil [13], experiencing urban stress makes people more susceptible to the chance of wrong personality traits because of epigenetic plasticity. Urban stresses that cause constant stress and inflammation in the body may result in changes in genes that control neurodevelopment and processing of emotions. This viewpoint is in line with the biopsychosocial model by incorporating brain functions, genetic links, and social or cultural aspects in explaining why personality disorders happen.

The combination of genetics, epigenetics, and neuroimaging gives a complete view of personality disorders. Genetic analysis paired with brain scanning has greatly helped us understand what happens physically in these illnesses. People who have the short serotonin transporter-linked promoter region (5-HTTLPR) polymorphism tend to experience larger changes in the amygdala when confronted with negative emotions, mainly if they have a history of early difficulties. Such analyses make it possible to detect biological markers that show the effects of genetic risk and may be targeted with treatments.

All in all, personality disorders are connected to various brain changes, imbalances in chemical levels, and interactions between genes and the environment. The results of these studies greatly affect the categories doctors use for diagnoses as well as their treatment methods. The introduction of the Research Domain Criteria (RDoC) and it indicates a new belief that personality disorders are terms for brain disorders that are clear in their pathophysiology. This way of thinking offers the possibility of creating treatments that relieve biology and address what happens in the brain to bring about these severe conditions.

4. Rethinking classification: Toward dimensional models

4.1 The limits of categorical diagnosis in personality disorders

More and more people now question whether the standard classification of personality disorders in the main sections of Diagnostic and Statistical Manual of

Mental Disorders, Fourth Edition (DSM-IV) and DSM-5 can identify the subtle details of someone's mental health problems. Part of the problem with the categorical model is the fixed use of separate and unconnected criteria, which do not fit the fact that different personality disorders can have common signs. A case in point is that Borderline Personality Disorder (BPD), Antisocial Personality Disorder (ASPD), and depressive personality traits usually occur together, showing related emotional and social problems, as well as similar forms of behavioral impulsiveness, harshness, and inability to feel empathy [9]. This kind of overlap makes it hard to tell the difference between distinct syndromes, sometimes causing situations where diagnoses cannot be settled and where comorbidity numbers grow. Many patients with unusual symptoms that lie outside the usual category may be underdiagnosed or mistreated. Since addressing these concerns was necessary, DSM-5-TR came with a different dimension-based model in Section III, which is another approach away from rigid categories [1]. Using this approach, it is recognized that personality difficulties involve a range of symptoms and can be managed with more flexibility. It adds various components by grouping five maladaptive personality traits—negative affectivity, detachment, antagonism, disinhibition, and psychoticism—that demonstrate the main aspects of a person's bad personality traits above categories (**Table 2**) [3].

4.2 The DSM-5-TR alternative model and trait-based diagnosis

Because of the AMPD in DSM-5-TR, clinicians can determine personality dysfunction by looking at both its type of expression and how severe it is. The Level of Personality Functioning Scale (LPFS) measures the problems that people with these disorders show in their thoughts and relationships with others. With the LPFS, the AMPD also finds maladaptive trait domains, which allow doctors to build a detailed

Key aspect	Description	Reference
Problem with Categorical Model	Uses fixed, separate criteria that do not account for overlapping symptoms among different personality disorders.	Spytska [9]
Symptom Overlap	Disorders such as BPD, ASPD, and depressive traits often share emotional, social, and behavioral patterns—e.g., impulsiveness, harshness, and lack of empathy.	Spytska [9]
Diagnosis Challenges	Overlapping symptoms lead to diagnostic uncertainty and high comorbidity rates.	Spytska [9]
Risk of Misdiagnosis	Atypical symptoms may not fit into any category, leading to underdiagnosis or mistreatment.	Spytska [9]
Response in DSM-5-TR	Section III introduces a dimensional model that moves beyond rigid categories to capture a broader range of personality dysfunction.	American Psychiatric Association [1]
Dimensional Model Traits	Five maladaptive traits: negative affectivity, detachment, antagonism, disinhibition, and psychoticism provide a more nuanced understanding of personality pathology.	Kolla et al. [3]
Flexibility of the New Model	Allows clinicians to evaluate personality disorders on a spectrum, improving diagnostic precision and treatment customization.	American Psychiatric Association [1]; Kolla et al. [3]

Table 2.
The limits of categorical diagnosis in personality disorders.

picture for every person. Under this approach, we realize that disinhibition in ASPD or negative affectivity in BPD might be part of many conditions and be shown in a variety of forms and at various degrees [1]. The DSM-5-TR makes it possible for clinicians to explain a patient's psychological issues in finer detail through traits. It means that scientists now focus on personality as a changing cluster of traits affected by what is happening in the brain, past experiences, and the social and cultural environment. They also mention that these forms of psychiatric classification are better connected to new findings in neuroimaging and molecular biology, offering support for more reliable diagnosing.

4.3 Trait qualifiers in ICD-11 and the move toward global harmonization

At the same time, the ICD-11 was created, parallel to the DSM-5-TR, using a dimensional model to describe personality disorders, reflecting the world's agreement that classification standards need upgrading. Personality disorders are now identified in ICD-11 by their severity as well as through traits, instead of being seen as individual categories. For example, these traits are negative affectivity, detachment, dissociability, disinhibition, and anaplastic, and they align with the main personality categories in the DSM-5-TR, but they continue to have their terms [2]. According to this model, personality disorder is seen as a range of faults in oneself and how they relate to others, which makes it easier to do sensitive individual evaluations, considering meaningful life, social, and mental factors. Using the guidelines from ICD-11, clinicians may explain a patient's personality problems using many different details, instead of just sticking to specific categories. With voice qualifiers, people's conditions can be traced and discussed over time, helping keep the diagnosis closer to real-world results. Equally important, having the DSM-5-TR and ICD-11 use similar dimensions is an indication of a movement toward uniformity in psychiatry around the world.

4.4 Integrating neurocognitive and biological markers into dimensional frameworks

Although the DSM-5-TR and ICD-11 dimensional models are more suitable and accurate, researchers say that combining neurocognitive issues and neurobiological signs could further improve the classification. Ruocco and Carcone [4] claim that connecting cognitive neuroscience with diagnosis could help explain the connection between mental ideas and brain processes. According to them, these disorders may be viewed as symptoms of problems in brain functions, including the inability to manage feelings, plan actions, and recognize others' mental states. In BPD, uncontrollable impulses and unstable feelings are due to problems in the frontolimbic region. At the same time, people with ASPD lack empathy and reason about right and wrong due to fewer activities in the orbitofrontal cortex and anterior cingulate area [3, 4]. Having these neurocognitive features in personality models allows us to relate them to biology and choose the best therapies. Also, Sahar [14] points out that key features, such as issues with empathy, problems in recognizing others, and troubles with emotions, are present in many personality disorders and show up as certain kinds of brain functioning. Such traits can be assessed with standard tools and brain scans so that they can be included in new psychiatric systems focused on blending different levels of brain, mind, and behavior.

4.5 Transdiagnostic traits and empathy dysregulation

Today's researchers in psychiatry increasingly believe that psychopathology is built on a few main traits. Among all the dysregulations, empathy dysregulation plays a significant role by crossing overdiagnosis and outlining standard processes in many personality disorders. With BPD, people experience deep feelings along with the inability to think about how others feel, which makes them react unpredictably and become overly frightened by being left out or rejected [7]. Differently, people with ASPD have fewer feelings of empathy, which leads to their being aggressive and morally uninterested as well [3]. According to Sahar [14], empathy should be considered as a range of linked thinking and feeling processes and not only as one single skill. It is possible to measure empathy dysregulation using tests, either by trying to recognize emotions or by how well someone matches what others feel. Because of these detection methods, therapists can better guide treatments, for example, through mental and social skills exercises or special drugs. Therefore, by including concepts like empathy in modern models, not only is the process of diagnosing patients enhanced but it also becomes easier to use personal and mechanism-oriented treatments [14].

4.6 Molecular signatures and epigenetic modulators of personality dimensions

Since psychiatry is going in the genetic direction, increasing evidence suggests that molecular and epigenetic markers can identify people's personalities and inform their dimensions. Galbiati [15] points out that in individuals with BPD and severe emotional and suicidal issues, there are specific alterations of molecules, for example, less brain-derived neurotrophic factor (BDNF) and problems with histone acetylation. Such biomarkers highlight the role of brain adaptation issues and disturbed gene expression in different cases of BPD. These molecular signatures are essential because they may cause difficulties in handling emotions and controlling impulses, supporting the reasons for each person's traits. Besides, when these biological markers are included in dimensional models, it produces a nosology that can be supported by evidence and used for treatment. Experts have used epigenetics to find out that early life challenges, along with other environmental hardships, can adjust our genes' activity by adding methyl groups or acetyl groups, making personality changes last over time [13]. Genes and a person's setting together provide a strong way to explain how some personality traits turn problematic and become more severe over time. If these studies are used in dimensional models, clinicians and researchers are able to create a taxonomy that reflects the links between a person's predisposition, their experiences, and how their brain functions [13, 15].

4.7 Implications for diagnosis, research, and clinical practice

The move from categorical to dimensional ways of classifying personality disorders significantly affects how researchers, doctors, and practitioners work. Because a dimensional approach can define each patient's complete profile, it becomes easier to plan a therapy process that fits their needs. With this new classification, clinicians can better notice how a person's characteristics develop with time and judge if the treatment is helping. When researchers consider brain and genetics, dimensional models offer measurable concepts that help research studies stay connected. Because of this, scientists can develop systems for classifying biomarkers and join different disciplines like neuroimaging and genomics. Besides, using transdiagnostic and neurocognitive approaches makes it easier to compare different disorders and discover the common reasons behind personality disorders, forming a coherent picture of the area [4, 14]. Looking at personality disorders as the result of complex traits allows us to use different therapies designed for specific individuals, for example, pharmacogenomics, neurofeedback, and cognitive remediation targeted at their needs. They are part of a bigger change called precision psychiatry, in which doctors and therapists take many factors unique to each person into account. Overall, the new way of looking at personality disorders is more than a change in classification and truly changes how we work with patients by bringing together science and clinical practice.

Seeking to use dimensional classification instead of defined categories is a key change in thinking and diagnosis for personality disorders. Acknowledging that just using categories causes confusion and relying instead on traits and neuroscience elements, both the DSM-5-TR and ICD-11 support more accurate and scientifically accurate ways to assess someone. The addition of neurocognitive problems, shared characteristics such as disturbances in empathy, and specific molecules such as BDNF and histone variations makes our understanding of personality pathology better. Employing these approaches in psychiatry is expected to increase diagnoses' accuracy, facilitate research done across several disciplines, and support the design of treatments that take individuals' needs into account. With the advancement of psychiatric nosology, seeing how neuroscience, trait-based theories, and clinical observations work together in the same framework may help clinicians and patients the most.

5. Neurobiologically informed interventions

With a better grasp of the brain aspects of personality disorders, more therapies based on neuroscience have appeared. They give top importance to the working structure of the brain and its connections with cognitive, emotional, and social parts, noting that the development and treatment of Borderline Personality Disorder (BPD), Antisocial Personality Disorder (ASPD), and depressive personality pathology need to consider biological, psychological, and environmental factors. Therefore, the use of strategies based on neurobiology has become essential in making successful interventions for each person. In this part, we study therapeutic approaches by examining cognitive and behavioral ways, drugs used in psychiatry, and novel neuromodulatory and biopsychosocial ways.

5.1 Cognitive and behavioral therapies

For quite some time, Cognitive-Behavioral Therapy (CBT) and Dialectical Behavior Therapy (DBT) have stood out as the main psychotherapeutic approaches for treating personality disorders, mostly BPD. Still, their success is improved when therapies are customized to match a person's brain abilities. Ellappan et al. [16] indicate that when CBT and DBT are designed for executive function, emotion management, and thinking skills unique to personality disorders, the success of the treatment rises. Clinicians now use pre-treatment assessments of patients' mental function, instead of following the same routines always. Example: If a patient has severe difficulties with memory, the usual way of cognitive therapy may not help, so it is better to employ methods that involve actively regulating behaviors when starting a new task [16].

In particular, DBT has been confirmed in studies to increase prefrontal regulation and, at the same time, reduce the high activation of areas such as the amygdala found in people with BPD and ASPD. Using neuroimaging techniques, Perez-Rodriguez et al. [17] showed that taking part in DBT for an extended period normalizes brain function and structure in the frontolimbic regions, which improves a person's emotional control. This therapy's goals of mindfulness, emotion control, coping with difficulty, and managing relationships seem to tune specific brain networks and, likewise, make people more responsive to emotions and better at thinking in a variety of social settings [17].

These changes in the brain are due to changes in molecules as well as their functions. Through DBT and other forms of psychotherapy, Galbiati [15] argues that meaningful changes in how the brain operates can take place at the level of cells, especially by bringing BDNF levels back to normal in people who suffer from mental health and personality problems. BDNF influences how neurons in the brain are connected, how people learn, and how memories form, and improvements in this growth factor may point to the benefit of behavioral therapy in reversing some changes in brain functions linked to personality problems. Based on this perspective, psychotherapists now focus on treatments that help create better and more stimulating surroundings, as well as connect strongly with their patients [15].

5.2 Pharmacologic approaches

Therapy is mainly used to treat most personality disorders, but medications can also be beneficial for dealing with sudden feelings, a lack of control, and aggressive acts. Still, most drug trials for personality disorders report mixed results, which might be partly because the symptoms and categories are not precisely defined. An impressive amount of research shows that SSRIs help manage main symptoms, such as emotional and behavioral changes common in BPD, ASPD, and other depressive personality disorders [11]. SSRIs act on serotonin in the brain to improve mood and reduce a person's emotional responses. Davis et al. [12] note that those who experience serotonin deficits often benefit from SSRIs since they help in the release of serotonin at synapses and influence the function of two regions in the brain related to controlling impulses and thinking about morals.

The use of mood stabilizers such as lithium and valproate has been investigated mainly because they regulate mood swings and lower impulsive behaviors. These medicines usually work better for individuals with mood disorders and strong fluctuations in mood than for people whose only issue is personality related. Among atypical antipsychotics, aripiprazole shows a remarkable ability to control hostility and aggression by targeting specific dopamine pathways. Instead of interfering with the brain's dopamine levels, as first-generation antipsychotics do, aripiprazole binds to dopamine (D2) and serotonin 1A (5-HT1A) receptors and blocks serotonin 2A (5-HT2A) receptors. It thus keeps anxiety and unwanted side effects to a minimum [3]. Researchers have found, through neuroimaging, that aripiprazole lessens emotional overreaction in the amygdala and increases control from the prefrontal parts of the brain. As a result, aripiprazole is supported as the best treatment for disorders with aggression and impulse issues [3].

Still, pharmacotherapy is not always sufficient whenever therapy and social support are not included. Since people have different responses, it makes sense that pharmacogenetic testing and using images from the brain in treatment could become usual practice. So far, we should continue to use a careful method for giving medications, paying attention to individuals' needs as well as the challenges involved in their complicated brains [11, 12].

5.3 Emerging neuromodulatory and biopsychosocial models

Over the last several years, several researchers have shown increased interest in targeting the brain circuits responsible for personality problems. A special mention is due to transcranial magnetic stimulation (TMS) since it can manage cortical excitability and stress in the prefrontal area associated with control over impulses and mood levels. They point out that specialized TMS to the dorsolateral prefrontal cortex is effective in strengthening mental control, managing inappropriate emotions, and supplying an alternative remedy for people who do not respond to usual therapy or medicine. Besides, early studies indicate that repeating TMS can improve the way the reward system and default mode network function together, which could help individuals with BPD and ASPD recover the ability to think about themselves and plan for the future [7].

As a new approach, mindfulness-based neurofeedback blends conventional meditation with updating brain signals to give people greater command over their brain functions. By using this approach, there is more communication between those parts of the brain related to identity and handling emotions. First, studies reveal that advanced integrative therapy (AIT) lowers impulsive actions and makes it easier for people to manage their emotions, most notably when this approach is supported by different kinds of psychotherapy [7]. They indicate a change in methods to tackle symptoms, as well as modify the brain structures that support unhealthy personality traits.

Studies suggest that modifications in brain function can be affected by factors in the environment and within society as well. According to Khalil [13], certain traits of our cities lead to neuroplastic overload and create more neurotoxins in the environment. In places where lots of people live close together, constant activation of the HPA axis can disturb the body's hormone levels, cause shrinking of the hippocampus, and intensify the emotional center of the brain, especially for those individuals who are at increased vulnerability. Urban planning, fairness in society, and workshops that teach about mental health are some of the policies Khalil [13] suggests, as these help reduce environmental dangers to mental health by bringing ecological psychiatry closer to neurobiology.

At the same time, Fidyk et al. [18] present a model that considers features of dissociation, trauma experienced, and the way the nervous system develops to understand personality disorders. It points out that the impact of many childhood hardships contributes to the slow development of the brain regions involved in feelings and planning. It points out that changes in the brain related to trauma often break the regular connections between areas involved in emotions and self-control, which can cause emotional difficulties, episodes of dissociation, and the formation of several different personalities in the same individual. In their paper, Fidyk et al. [18] support using trauma-informed methods that fit with development and that ensure safety in relationships, as well as body awareness, since change in therapy can happen through the development of coherent and integrated patterns in the brain.

All in all, the area is progressing toward using multiple types of treatments that involve studies from neuroscience, drugs, social psychology, and public health.
To sum up, this vision is based on further exploring personality disorders through Cognitive-Behavioral Therapy, neuromodulatory technologies, precise use of drugs,

and ecological psychiatry [13, 15, 16, 18]. This way of thinking about personality pathology sees it as the result of the brain, mind, and environment working together, so experts have to use all available scientific tools to address it.

6. Research gaps and future directions

Although scientists have made good progress in understanding how personality disorders affect the brain, there are still many unanswered questions that block further improvements in using the right treatments. A primary obstacle is there is not a specific biomarker that can accurately spot the difference between different personality disorders. There are many reports from neuroimaging and molecular studies mentioning how abnormalities in the amygdala or connections between the prefrontal and limbic areas occur in depression. Still, they are too inconsistent across people to be used by themselves as diagnostic tools [6]. Since there is a constant gap despite studies, it shows that PD has many forms, and there is an urgent need for biomarkers to account for the interactions between a person's genes, what they experience in life, and brain changes.

Moreover, researchers in the field still lack much longitudinal data that can describe exactly how early brain problems in young individuals turn into the traits of Parkinson's disease as people grow up. These current techniques provide only one picture of personality and do not let us watch for changes in people's conditions with time. Such studies are beneficial for identifying critical periods like adolescence when changes in the brain and hormones might lead to changes in an individual's risk factors [5]. A lack of such data makes it hard to spot the best moments to help through early intervention, and as a result, practical prevention measures may be put off.

It is just as important to point out that few papers focus on how cultural, social, and environmental factors impact health. Although having high levels of trauma, adversity, and urban living can make an essential difference in PDs, these factors are still considered unimportant by most neuropsychiatric treatment models [13]. Since cities have more stressors and some people are less able to deal with them, it is urgent to research the idea that chronic stress can interfere with the brain's functioning [8]. As long as there are no customized models, it results in unfair diagnoses and a lack of usable evidence for various countries. Hence, studies in the future need to analyze the connections between society and the environment to see how environmental and cultural influences affect the brain development of children.

Research on future PD management needs to use a range of techniques, such as fMRI, electroencephalography (EEG), and diffusion tensor imaging (DTI), as well as look at genetic material and advanced psychological tests. When these domains are connected, researchers can detect functional biological and behavioral characteristics in PDs, which help identify patients earlier and correctly. This way, specialists might develop individual plans through a person's distinct brain, genetic, and psychological characteristics. For the progress of research and treatment in personality pathology, it is now imperative to use multiple types of research, examine subjects for a long time, and take cultural differences into account [15].

7. Conclusion

All in all, personality disorder research is being revolutionized by using an approach that links mental, physical, and genetic aspects. By exceeding the kind of checklist aimed at a simple diagnosis, modern models now notice that many PDs show a spectrum of features. Thus, not only is it a more accurate method, but it also agrees with how these disorders usually develop and what is found at a molecular level. Because proof is accumulating about problems in the nervous system, imbalances in brain messengers, and gene and environment influences, more support is given to a single biology-based diagnostic approach. It is essential to see that helpful intervention depends on knowing who to target and when to do it, as development is not the same for everyone. The use of new technologies and techniques has the ability to open a new period in psychiatry where personality pathology is recognized as a real biological condition that can be studied, predicted, and treated. Progress in medicine adds to the possibility of more considerate and helpful treatments for patients with these serious and human illnesses.

Author details

Hafiz Shafique Ahmad[1*] and Khizra Mussadiq[2]

1 Department of Psychiatry, DGKHAN Medical College Dera Ghazi Khan, Punjab, Pakistan

2 Nishtar Hospital Multan, Pakistan

*Address all correspondence to: drhshafiq@ymail.com

References

[1] American Psychiatric Association. Diagnostic and Statistical Manual of Mental Disorders. 5th ed. Text Rev. (DSM-5-TR). Washington, DC: American Psychiatric Association Publishing; 2022

[2] World Health Organization. International Classification of Diseases. 11th ed. Geneva: World Health Organization; 2022. Available from: https://icd.who.int/

[3] Kolla NJ, Tully J, Bertsch K. Neural correlates of aggression in personality disorders from the perspective of DSM-5 maladaptive traits: A systematic review. Translational Psychiatry. 2023;**13**:330. DOI: 10.1038/s41398-023-02612-1

[4] Ruocco AC, Carcone D. A neurobiological model of borderline personality disorder: Systematic and integrative review. Harvard Review of Psychiatry. 2016;**24**(5):311-329. DOI: 10.1097/HRP.0000000000000114

[5] Paris J. The neurobiology and genetics of borderline personality disorder. Psychiatric Clinics of North America. 2020;**43**(1):1-11. DOI: 10.1016/j.psc.2019.10.001

[6] Schmaal L, Veltman DJ, van Erp TGM, Sämann PG, Hibar DP. Imaging genetics in psychiatry—Advances and future directions. Nature Reviews Neuroscience. 2020;**21**(7):371-388. DOI: 10.1038/s41583-020-0314-5

[7] Herpertz SC, Bertsch K. A new perspective on the pathophysiology of borderline personality disorder: A model of the role of oxytocin. American Journal of Psychiatry. 2014;**171**(8):820-828. DOI: 10.1176/appi.ajp.2014.13121615

[8] Rheude C, Nikendei C, Stopyra MA, Bendszus M, Krämer B, Gruber O, et al. Two sides of the same coin? What neural processing of emotion and rewards can tell us about complex post-traumatic stress disorder and borderline personality disorder. Journal of Affective Disorders. 2024;**368**:711-719. DOI: 10.1016/j.jad.2024.09.110

[9] Spytska L. Anxiety and depressive personality disorders in the modern world. Acta Psychologica. 2024;**246**:104285-104285. DOI: 10.1016/j.actpsy.2024.104285

[10] D'Adda F, Sighinolfi G, Mitolo M, Scala M, Guidi L, Motta L, et al. Neurobiological correlates of personality dimensions in borderline personality disorder using graph analysis of functional connectivity. Scientific Reports. 2025;**15**:12623. DOI: 10.1038/s41598-025-85989-x

[11] Coccaro EF, Lee R, McCloskey MS. Serotonin and impulsive aggression. Journal of Psychiatric Research. 2011;**45**(6):791-798. DOI: 10.1016/j.jpsychires.2011.01.004

[12] Davis MT, Asch RH, Weiss ER, Wagner A, Fineberg SK, Nabulsi N, et al. An in vivo examination of the relationship between metabotropic glutamate 5 receptor and suicide attempts in people with borderline personality disorder. Biological Psychiatry: Cognitive Neuroscience and Neuroimaging. 2024;**10**(3):324-332. DOI: 10.1016/j.bpsc.2024.11.014

[13] Khalil MH. Borderline in a linear city: Urban living brings borderline personality disorder to crisis through neuroplasticity—an urgent call to action. Frontiers in Psychiatry. 2025;**15**:1524531. DOI: 10.3389/fpsyt.2024.1524531

[14] Ghalebin SSA. A neuroscience perspective on antisocial personality

disorder (ASPD). Applied Psychology Research. 2024;**3**(2):1439. DOI: 10.59400/apr.v3i2.1439

[15] Galbiati C. Borderline Personality Disorder: Molecular Signatures Linked to Pathology and Psychotherapy Effects. Italy: Uniecampus.it; 2025. Available from: https://hdl.handle.net/11389/67178

[16] Ellappan S, Subba R, Mondal AC. Understanding borderline personality disorder: Clinical features, neurobiological insights, and therapeutic strategies. Progress in Neuro-Psychopharmacology and Biological Psychiatry. 2025;**139**:111403. DOI: 10.1016/j.pnpbp.2025.111403

[17] Perez-Rodriguez MM, Bulbena-Cabré A, Bassir Nia A, Zipursky G, Goodman M, New AS. The neurobiology of borderline personality disorder. Psychiatric Clinics of North America. 2018;**41**(4):633-650. DOI: 10.1016/j.psc.2018.07.012

[18] Fidyk M, Bolek M, Jagieła B, Kędzia A, Musialska D, Minkiewicz M. Dissociative identity disorder: A comprehensive review of Etiology, diagnosis, neurobiology, and treatment. Quality in Sport. 2025;**41**:60277. DOI: 10.12775/qs.2025.41.60277

Chapter 2

Perspective Chapter: Motivation of Criminal Behavior in Secondary School Students in Chihuahua City, Northern Mexico

Joel Monárrez-Espino, Luisa Villareal-Varela, Estefanía Pinzón-Kranz, Lorena Ávila-Carrasco, Margarita Martínez-Fierro and Jesús Vaca-Cortés

Abstract

Qualitative study with secondary school adolescents (~14–15 years) in the city of Chihuahua to identify motivators of criminal behavior. In-depth interviews were conducted using individual interview guides. Data were recorded, transcribed, and coded by thematic axes. The main reason for carrying weapons was for protection and safety when living in isolated dangerous areas. The motivation for physical aggression included self-defense or defense of family and friends, out of impulsiveness, as reaction to insults or mistreatment, to gain respect, and as an act of manliness. Using alcohol or drugs was relatively common among students from poor schools, especially men; curiosity or peer pressure was mentioned, as well as positive sensations that help combat stress, anxiety and depression, and family problems. Motivation for stealing included doing it as a prank and due to the influence or pressure from friends. Belonging to gangs had to do with the desire to be respected, to have prestige and protection, due to influence by friends or brothers, or to feel part of something. Crime behavior appears to be a problem among high-risk groups in poor and marginalized areas of the city; preventive efforts should be focused on vulnerable students.

Keywords: behavior, criminal, Mexico, secondary school, student

1. Introduction

The increase and recurrence of crimes committed by minors in Mexico, including robbery, kidnapping, and even homicide, has been viewed with great concern [1]. The state of Chihuahua, located in northern Mexico, has stood out as not only one of the states where most adolescents are involved in crimes but also one where they are the most victims of organized crime [2].

Since school is a key environment during adolescence, a probabilistic survey was conducted with 430 students from 41 secondary schools in the city of Chihuahua in 2020 to determine the prevalence of antisocial and criminal behaviors, and to identify associated risk factors [3]. This study showed that spending money on gambling (17.2%), damaging public objects or property (15.5%), and stealing objects or money from automatic devices (11.6%) were the most common delinquent behaviors. Men were observed to have a higher average score for criminal behaviors compared with women (1.35 vs. 0.89; $p < 0.05$), and 3rd year secondary school students (9th grade for international comparisons) had higher averages than 1st and 2nd year students (1.44 vs. 0.98 and 0.94; $p < 0.05$).

It was also observed that having failed at least one previous school year was associated with higher mean criminal scores compared with never having failed (1.91 vs. 1.04; $p < 0.05$). Notably, not reporting family problems (0.70) and spending time with family as the most common free-time activity (0.67) resulted in the lowest mean criminal scores. Regarding school type, telesecundarias (broadcast TV schools that provide distance education), common in the most socioeconomically marginalized areas, had the highest mean criminal score (2.31). When the risk of engaging in at least one criminal behavior was assessed using multivariate logistic regression, the lowest tertile of academic performance vs. the highest was associated with a higher likelihood (adjusted odds ratio 3.52; 95% confidence interval 1.63–7.59), as was reporting family problems vs. not having (3.05; 1.55–6.02), and being in 3rd vs. 1st year of secondary school (2.39; 1.43–3.99). Notably, meeting with family had a protective effect compared with participating in social media, watching TV, playing video games, or meeting with friends [3].

While that survey laid the quantitative foundation for identifying the distribution and frequency of antisocial and criminal behavior, the results obtained did not capture the motivations behind such conducts. Why do these adolescents engage in these behaviors? What motivates them to steal, physically assault someone, carry a knife, or use drugs? What reasons lead to or trigger such behaviors? These are questions that can only be answered by giving voice to those who engage in those actions. For this reason, a qualitative approach was used based on in-depth interviews with students who reported having engaged in criminal acts.

Therefore, this study aimed at identifying motivators of criminal behaviors of adolescent school students in the city of Chihuahua. The research protocol of this study was reviewed and approved by the Ethics and Research Committees at Christus Muguerza Hospital of Chihuahua city (ID: HCMP-CEI-25072022). Authorization was given by participating schools. Informed consent was obtained from parents or guardians after the students' assent.

2. Methodology

A qualitative ethnographic study [4, 5] focused on 9th grade junior high school students (3rd year of secondary school in the Mexican system) from public and private schools in the city of Chihuahua who reported having engaged in five or more criminal behaviors.

2.1 School selection

A convenience sampling was used based on the results obtained in the representative survey conducted previously [3]. The objective was to maximize the probability that the selected school had students who engage in criminal behaviors. Initially, the 41 schools sampled in that survey were ranked from the largest to the smallest proportion of respondents who reported ≥1 criminal behavior out of the total enrollment of the school. Then, from the first 10 schools ranked, five were purposely selected taking into consideration the following criteria: (a) the school had to have >150 students, (b) the percentage of students surveyed out of the total enrollment was >1.5%, (c) at least one school from each type of secondary school had to be included (general public, technical public, telesecundaria, and private), and (d) the school authorities had to agree to participate. Thus, the following five schools were selected.

2.1.1 Southern public school (SPS)

This was a morning-shift school located south of the city in a dangerous and marginalized area of a low socioeconomic status. Most parents had basic education (up to high school); many work in assembly plants. The school had 559 students (48% female, 52% male) and 24 teachers. Of 165 students in the five 9th grade groups, 112 participated in the screening survey (response rate: 68%). The reception by the authorities and teachers was cordial, but the atmosphere among the students was difficult; insults were constantly heard, and physical fights were witnessed between some students.

2.1.2 Northern technical school (NTS)

This was a morning-shift public technical school located northwest of the city in a middle-class area. It was the only school selected with students with some type of disability. The school's administrators and teachers expressed interest in participating in the study. The school had 491 students (47% female, 53% male) and 17 teachers. Of the 158 students in the four 9th grade groups, 101 participated in the survey (response rate: 64%). The teachers knew the students well. Artistic and musical activities were promoted. School officials stated that when a student had psychological or behavioral problems, he or she was referred to other agencies.

2.1.3 Southern telesecundaria (STV)

This was a morning-shift public school located in a semirural, marginalized southern area of the city of a low socioeconomic status. There were 248 registered students (43% female, 57% male) and 12 teachers. Of the 73 students in the two 9th grade groups, 46 completed the survey (response rate: 64%). Parents' educational background was low (few had completed secondary school). Most worked in assembly plants and in the construction industry; some were unemployed. The environment was problematic, both students and staff. Absenteeism among students and teachers was common. Problems of sexual abuse were also reported.

2.1.4 Private secondary school (PSS)

This was a morning-shift private bilingual school of middle-upper class status located in the city center. The school environment was friendly and respectful. The students were somewhat reserved but engaged. There were 178 registered students (53% female, 47% male) and 15 teachers. Of the 105 students in four 9th grade groups, 43 participated in the screening survey (response rate: 41%). Several parents did not agree to participate.

2.1.5 Northern public school (NPS)

This was a middle/low-income morning-shift school located in the north of the city. Given the limited budget, the community often provides in-kind support to improve the school's operations. It had 248 students (47% female, 53% male) and 12 teachers. Of the 46 students in the three 9th grade groups, 33 completed the survey (response rate: 71%). Officials reported that they frequently received students who were rejected or expelled from other schools. The teachers knew the students well; they reported an increase in insecurity and vandalism in and around the school.

2.2 Antisocial and criminal behavior questionnaire

This validated Spanish questionnaire explores antisocial and criminal dimensions [6]. Participants respond dichotomously to the 20 questions on each scale, for a final score ranging from 0 to 20 points for each dimension. The questions on the antisocial scale address behaviors that demonstrate lack of compliance with social norms; for example: Do you litter the streets or sidewalks by breaking bottles or throwing trash cans? Do you paint graffiti in prohibited places? Have you been involved in fights with others by punching, insulting, or using offensive language? Criminal behaviors refer to behaviors that may have legal consequences; for example: Have you broken into a warehouse, garage, or store? Have you tried to escape from the police or fought with a police officer? Have you stolen things from businesses when they are open? Do you use or take drugs? This instrument has shown a Cronbach's alpha of 0.90, which is considered a reliable coefficient of internal consistency. This study used the version adapted for use in the Mexican population [7], which has also been applied in other populations previously [8, 9].

2.3 Selection of informants

Given that the mean score and prevalence of antisocial and criminal behaviors were higher among 9th grade students, the sampling strategy focused on these adolescents. The selected schools were first visited by the researchers. Upon request and authorization from school authorities, the antisocial and criminal questionnaire was administered to all 9th grade students in the five schools selected (n = 320) under informed consent from parents/guardians, and assent from the students themselves [10]. Those who reported ≥5 criminal behaviors were eligible for in-depth interviews; this screening method led to a total of 21 students eligible, of whom only one female student refused to participate, leaving a total of 20 interviews (SPS 8, NTS 5, STV 4, PSS 2, NPS 1). The sampling strategy for the entire study, including phases 1 (quantitative) and 2 (qualitative), is illustrated in **Figure 1**.

2.4 General interview guide

First, a semi-structured interview guide was designed, grouping the questions from the AD questionnaire into 8 relevant topics: (1) vandalizing, littering, or damaging things and places; (2) entering prohibited places; (3) stealing other people's property; (4) disrespect toward others; (5) physical and verbal violence; (6) gang membership and carrying weapons; (7) drinking, drugs, and gambling; and (8) defiance of authority.

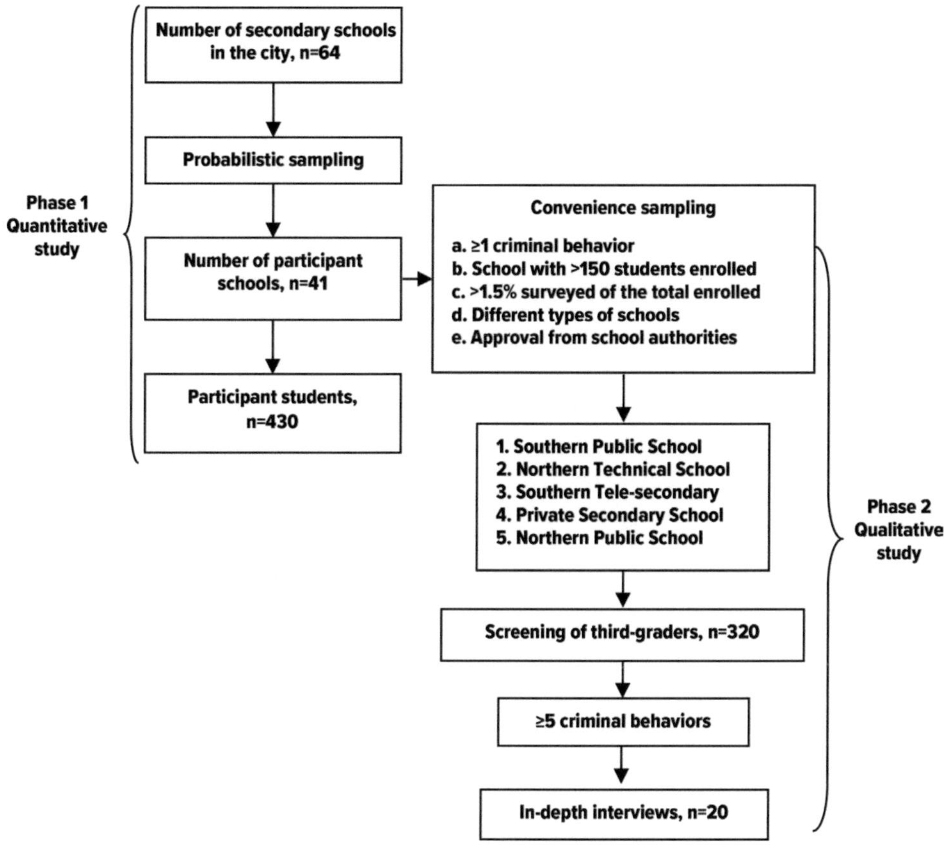

Figure 1.
Sampling strategy of the study on antisocial and criminal behavior among secondary school students of the City of Chihuahua, Mexico.

Antisocial behaviors (A) and criminal (C) behaviors were classified within the corresponding topic. For example, for the topic of "entering prohibited places," the following behaviors were grouped: entering a prohibited place such as a private garden or empty house (A); breaking into a warehouse, garage, or store (C); entering a club or purchasing prohibited drinks (C); and entering a closed store even if nothing is stolen (C). Then, the interview question and follow-up guide were designed to address this issue. For the previous example, the questions included: Have you ever entered a forbidden place (home, closed store, nightclub, etc.)? Tell me about the occasion when you did this. Who were you with? How often do you do it? Why did you decide to do it? Why do you keep doing it? How do you feel when you do it? How did you feel afterwards?

2.5 In-depth interviews

For in-depth interviews [11, 12], a second informed consent was obtained from parents or guardians, as well as the student's assent, explaining the purpose and confidentiality of the interview. Students' characteristics, including school, family, and students' personal situation, are presented in **Table 1**. The interviews lasted 45–60 minutes; they were recorded and conducted by three trained interviewers.

			Situation					
ID	Sex	Code	School	Family			Personal	
			Characteristics	Lives with	Reports problems	Has failed in school	Works now	Preferred activity
1	M	SPS-A	General, public, south, lower income	Father	Few	No	No	Friends
2	F	SPS-B		Mother	Many	Yes	No	Friends
3	M	SPS-C		Both	Some	No	No	Friends
4	F	SPS-D		Both	Few	No	No	Social media
5	M	SPS-E		Mother	Many	No	Yes	Friends
6	M	SPS-F		Both	None	No	No	TV-video
7	M	SPS-G		Both	None	No	No	TV-video
8	M	SPS-H		Mother	Some	No	Yes	Friends
9	F	NTS-A	Technical, public, north, middle income	Mother	Few	No	No	Social media
10	F	NTS-B		Both	None	No	No	Sports
11	F	NTS-C		Mother	Many	No	No	Social media
12	M	NTS-D		Mother	Few	Yes	No	Friends
13	M	NTS-E		Both	Some	No	Yes	Sports
14	M	STV-A	Telesec undaria, public, south, lower income	Both	None	Yes	No	Friends
15	M	STV-B		Others	None	No	Yes	Sports
16	F	STV-C		Mother	Few	No	No	Sports
17	M	STV-D		Mother	None	No	No	Sports
18	F	PSS-A	General, private, center, upper-middle income	Both	Few	No	No	Family
19	F	PSS-B		Mother	Few	No	No	Sports
20	M	NPS-A	General, public, north, middle-lower income	Mother	Some	No	No	Sports

M: Male, F: Female.

Table 1.
Characteristics of students interviewed according to their school, family and personal situation.

They were conducted in a private location within the school premises during class time. The school was visited prior to the interviews to familiarize interviewers with the school facilities and staff. A 5-minute rapport-building period was used with each respondent before recording. Thereafter, the motivations behind the behaviors reported by each student were addressed. Field notes were taken during the interview process to enhance the analysis [13].

2.6 Interview transcription, coding, and analysis

Content analysis [14] was used to systematically code and identify motivations using an inductive approach. First, the interviews were transcribed verbatim. Open codes were then generated inductively by the researchers, as well as *in vivo* codes based on participants' statements to avoid losing the intended meaning. These codes addressed the following thematic axes considered most relevant from a criminal perspective: carrying or using weapons, physical violence, alcohol and drugs, theft, gang membership, problems with the police, organized crime, and family issues. The codes were grouped and organized to form categories based on their common meaning.

Motivations for the reported behaviors were then identified, and axial coding was performed by systematically searching for the relationships between codes and categories until theoretical saturation was achieved. Excerpts were used to illustrate the motivation behind the behaviors reported by the interviewed students. The aim was to prioritize the presentation of quotes that best illustrated the incentive for engaging in behaviors within each area addressed.

3. Results

Table 2 presents the mean scores for criminal behaviors of 9th grade students from the five selected schools in the city of Chihuahua used for individual sampling screening according to student characteristics. Mean scores for criminal behaviors were slightly higher among men compared with women, but no statistical significance was reached (1.45 vs. 1.20; $p > 0.05$). Having failed at least one previous year was associated with a nonsignificant higher mean score compared with never having failed (1.63 vs. 1.29; $p > 0.05$). In terms of the students' residence, living with both parents resulted in one of the lowest mean criminal scores, especially when compared with living with the mother only, reaching statistical significance (1.02 vs. 1.76; $p < 0.05$). On the other hand, not living with either parent resulted in the highest mean criminal score (2.42), while living with both parents showed the lowest criminal score (1.02). Family gatherings as a preferred leisure activity also had a protective effect, reflected in the lowest mean criminal score in the entire analysis (0.76). Reporting many family problems had the highest mean score (3.00), while not reporting any family problems had the lowest mean in the family problem analysis (0.95). These results are very similar to the previously published in the probabilistic cross-sectional survey conducted earlier with 430 adolescents from 41 secondary schools of the city of Chihuahua [3].

Regarding the school context, staff at the poorest and most marginalized schools reported frequent fights and conflicts as well as situations involving drug use or serious problems that led to student suspension or transfer to other institutions. References to parents who were disinterested in their children's development and problems were common, especially in poor schools, citing their lack of time due to work responsibilities to support their families.

The results are presented according to the thematic axes of the interviews. Approximately one-third of the students accounted for a substantial portion of the quotes used in this section, as they were the ones who engaged in the most relevant behaviors.

Characteristic	Category	n	Mean (s.d.)*
Sex	Male	135	1.45 ± 2.07
	Female	171	1.20 ± 1.76
Failed a previous year	Never	287	1.29 ± 1.86
	At least once	19	1.63 ± 2.54
Family situation	Does not live with parents	12	2.42 ± 2.31
	Lives with father	9	1.56 ± 2.18
	Lives with mother	94	1.76 ± 2.31[a]
	Lives with both parents	189	1.02 ± 1.57[b]
Reports family problems	None	148	0.95 ± 1.62[a]
	Few	80	146 ± 1.98
	Some	64	1.66 ± 1.73[b]
	Many	12	3.00 ± 3.76[b]
Free time activity	Meeting with family	37	0.76 ± 1.18
	Play sports	85	1.52 ± 1.90
	Social networks	28	136 ± 1.94
	TV and videogames	69	1.29 ± 1.85
	Going out with friends	83	1.41 ± 2.20
Works currently	No	266	1.27 ± 1.83
	Yes	39	1.62 ± 2.36
Total		302	1.33 ± 1.91

[1]*Convenience sample of 5 schools: 2 general public, 1 public technical 1 telesecondary, and 1 private.*
**Student's t-test and ANOVA with Tukey comparisons; different subscripts indicate statistical difference ($p < 0.05$).*

Table 2.
Mean score of criminal behaviors of 9th grade students in the five secondary schools[1] selected for individual sampling screening according to student characteristics.

3.1 Carrying/using weapons

Those who reported this behavior primarily referred to bladed weapons, although a couple mentioned other types ("boxer"–an iron weapon–and gun). Those who carried or used weapons were from public secondary schools, particularly those located in the marginalized southern part of the city (telesecundaria and general secondary schools). The primary motivations included a sense of protection and self-defense, and avoiding assaults. Others reported being encouraged to carry weapons by family members, and some even normalized carrying such weapons. A couple of students mentioned hiding their bladed weapons so that they would not be detected at school during searches.

A telesecundaria [STV-C] female student reported that her mother was afraid and supported her carrying a knife for her safety given the danger in the area: "*...knives and butterfly knives, yes, in fact, sometimes I carry one because I go back alone, so the way things are right now I have to carry it... these days there's a lot of that, girls being robbed, girls being raped, and all that; so I carry that for safety.*" Regarding her mother's promotion of carrying a knife, she mentioned: "*..yes, what happens is that my mom has always* *told me to carry it. And more so because if I go back alone, then she's afraid something will happen to me."* Regarding carrying the weapon, she added: *"...noooo, well, I mean, I feel good; I feel empowered* [she said it mockingly]."

Another student [SPS-E] mentioned carrying knives and firearms, arguing necessity, and even referred having used a gun: *"Knives, a gun, right now I have the...* [points to his hand and takes out a knife and a boxer –an iron device–]*...yes, yes I have one, or sometimes I have, usually when I go out on the street and so on; knives or sometimes a gun in case is needed."* When asked if he had ever used them, he responded: *"Yes, I've done a lot, yes I've done a lot..."* [laughs, implying that he has shot and pointing with his hand in the shape of a gun]. He then added: *"...I also stabbed a guy once."*

Another student [SPS-A] mentioned carrying weapons for security reasons due to his parents' separation: *"...since my dad and mom split, I have to go to my mom's house, so I have to carry weapons because the road is very dangerous, so, for self-defense."*

3.2 Physical violence

Physical, verbal, and psychological violence was reported. Emphasis was placed on physical violence actively inflicted by students rather than on violence against them. The focus was on fights/arguments with others, such as classmates, friends, family members, and strangers. Fights were justified as defending someone weaker (e.g., a younger brother from the mother, a mother from the stepfather, or a fragile classmate), due to an aggressive personality or for being impulsive, as a reaction to harassment or anger caused by a previous action (e.g., being insulted or mistreated), as an act of manliness, as an act of self-defense, and to gain respect. Several students reported seeing their family members fight, and some even received fighting lessons from brothers, fathers, or uncles.

Violent behavior was reported by both men and women but was far less common in the private high school. Some students reported frequent street fights. Very few reported feeling remorse after the fight. One student made homophobic comments to justify the attacks.

Regarding family influence, a student from a public school said [SPS-E]: *"Oh yeah! My dad was a real brawler, a real buscarruidos* [a troublemaker who causes conflicts] *and he didn't let anyone take advantage of him, he even got into fights with the police or something like that; he didn't care, and I think that's why I also have this fight thing going on, especially because of my dad and my family... yeah, my brother is a real brawler too, my brother was here, he was expelled during his first year."*

A female student [SPS-B] referred to an argument in the neighborhood where she lives, which ended in a report to the prosecutor's office: "*When I arrived... I was already angry... I already had a lot of things on my plate, because I was also in a lot of trouble with other classmates... I pushed her, but well, it got all tangled up and that's it... she started pulling my hair and that's when I hit her and I ripped out a lot of her hair... and her mom hit me too and I hit her mom back and that's it... it was because more than anything the mom raised her hand to me and my brother too... we already had a lot of problems with them because they also kept scolding my older sister and things like that and my mom went to file the complaint that same day. And they called both families together and they started talking, and then the mother got angry and wanted to hit me again...*" Referring to herself, she said: *"I have a very strong temper. My mom says I have a very strong temper. So, we got to the point of hitting more than anything. So, then it continued in the school... they had me classified as a problem child and that's why I didn't do well, in second year* [of secondary]."

In a fight between classmates at the telesecundaria, a student [STV-C] stated the following: *"...and she started telling me that she was never going to apologize to me and that I was a hypocrite and that I said a lot of things about her and who knows what else... she stood up and pushed me and well, at that moment I went blind. I grabbed her and threw her to the ground; I had her strangled. And well, she has a sister. And the moment her sister saw this, well, she jumped on me and I grabbed her too and slammed her to the ground and I said to her: 'You move over there, the problem isn't with you.' And when I stood up, because she told me to get out of the way, I also got angry and hit her, I gave her another... another blow to the face... up to now she keeps telling me that she beat me* [in the fight] *and that she really is after me* [to get revenge] *ever since I hit her sister and so... yes, I have that character to fight, but not that much."*

A student [SPS-E], referring to family influence, said: *"...since I was little, I was with my brother, and he talked to me a lot about fights. Since then I really like fighting, for example, there was a time where the first fights I saw where my dad and my uncle fought scared me, but with time it goes away and I was the one fighting, but ever since I was little, in elementary school it was me who fought and stuff, I was one of the ones who started fight..."*. Regarding whether he continued fighting, he said: *"Yes, once I had to kick a kid in the butt and stuff like that... I now hardly get involved anymore... if someone is doing something to me, I deal with that alone, but if somebody needs help, I'll also get involved."*

A student from a public school [NPS-A], when asked why he had fought, said: *"No, because they said that I had a voice like, a voice like something... like a whistle* [very high-pitched, but in slang it also means penis], *that's what they told me... And then, at first, I let it go, but then it was when they started shouting that word out loud, that's when I came back* [to fight]."

A student from the technical school mentioned having fought to defend family members: *"...he messed with my family, he told them* [the other students] *that they were blind* [there are blind people in his family]*; that's when I really got angry...and the boy almost ended up in the hospital from the blows* [he received from him]." When asked why he had reacted that way, he responded: *"...well, it was like an impulse, it wasn't planned. When he said: 'wherever I see you, I'm going to hurt you', I told him I wasn't afraid...then I ran into him outside...he hadn't even looked up at me or anything...that's when the impulse kicked in...and because of everything he had said, then I pushed him. I asked him to repeat what he had told in that message* [that he had texted it]. *And then I started to hit him."*

3.3 Alcohol and drugs

Alcohol use was mentioned by several students, but drug use was reported by only a few students, primarily men. Marijuana ("mota" in local slang) was the most frequently mentioned illicit drug, although three students also referred to the use or sale of methamphetamines ("tachas" in local slang), "wax" (marijuana extract in wax form), cocaine, and medications such as clonazepam (a benzodiazepine), and "mona" (toluene-containing inhalants). Alcohol and drug use were cited for relaxation, to forget problems (including family problems), to socialize, to concentrate, out of curiosity, to address stress, insomnia, depression, to avoid feelings and responsibilities, and because they generated positive feelings and happiness.

Some reported having received consent to consume alcohol at family gatherings, but it was reported that both alcohol and drugs were used mostly secretly, at parties and on weekends, with friends and in gangs. Very few reported feelings of anxiety or fear of being exposed, or remorse for having used them. Two students reported getting involved in drug dealing because their father was a drug dealer, and because there were "picaderos" (drug houses) in their neighborhood. Drug use was not reported at the private school, but alcohol and tobacco were used at parties where older students bring alcohol and cigarettes to gain popularity.

A student [SPS-E] said about buying marijuana: "*…and I asked where I could get it, and they gave me the contact, and I went and bought it, and then I went with some friends and from there we started* [consuming it]."

A student from the telesecundaria [STV-A] referring to marijuana said: "*…at a party they gave me little bags of marijuana and I was looking after them. One of the guys who was with me opened it and the weed fell out… they wanted to hit me, but one guy took out a BB gun and started a fight. They told me to leave and someone came on a motorcycle for me… and about an hour later they told me that they had killed someone…*" Regarding drug sales, he said: "*…they get them like this on a street, behind mine, they are called picaderos* (drug houses), *there are like three on the same street and like this on the other street there are two others, and there on one of those they sell mota* [marijuana] *and tachas* [methamphetamines] *and I don't remember what else, they get it there.*"

Another student [SPS-A] refers to consuming alcohol and drugs like this: "*..yes, with some friends we went to a bar and just… to drink and be with friends…*" About using drugs: "*…well, weed, wax* [marijuana extract] *and mona* [inhalants]*…I would like to talk about drugs because at the time they really calmed my anxiety and stress because of biting my nails and stuff. I never got to the point of cutting myself or thinking about suicide, no, nothing like that, I have never reached that point, and I hope I never do, honestly. Drugs did me good for a moment and bad for the next, and obviously I didn't use them because, 'Oh, I want to!' No, the vice! No, I used them when I felt bad, so that something would help me…I thought they helped me in the sense that they calmed me down, but from then on they did hurt me…right now I have used, not much, to be honest, but I have used and not in large quantities, like a joint, you could say that one hit and that's it, and that's only when I go out, but only from then on, nothing more.*"

A female telesecundaria student [STV-C] reports that her father was a drug dealer: "*…my dad doesn't let me say it, it's just that my dad… used to sell drugs, because he doesn't sell anymore. And since he trusts me a lot, he told me: 'when you see…* [hesitates whether to continue speaking] *… give it to me or hide it' because he lived with my grandmother and no, my grandmother doesn't like that.*" When asked if she had used drugs, she replied that it does not bother her "*…because I've seen a lot of people like that, well, on drugs, and I say, I wouldn't like to be in that situation.*"

Another female student [SPS-D] referred to the use of benzodiazepines like this: "*…some pills, clonazepam they are called… it was very little, but my sister was the one found out because my pupils were very dilated… she didn't tell my parents anything, but that's why it started from there, we went to the hospital because I fainted and they realized the problem with my heart.*"

Another student [STV-B] also referred to marijuana and cocaine use: "*…I used to work because I didn't like being at home, so I worked Monday through Sunday, sometimes from 8 a.m. to 7 p.m., or sometimes from 8 a.m. to 2 p.m. or so. So, everyone was like, 'Do you want some drugs?' and everyone did. Then there was a moment when they pressured me too much, and I did it… it was marijuana and cocaine.*" When asked about her experience of using marijuana, she said: "*The truth is, I felt better. I don't know. Well, since it was my first time, I actually felt kind of weird, but I stopped thinking about all of that so much and I was, I felt happy, I felt different. But I didn't do it again because I quit the job. When I analyzed the situation and saw that what I was doing was too bad, that I could get into too much trouble doing that. And I quit. The truth is, I liked it.*"

Another student [SPS-B] said he had used marijuana excessively and had quit out of fear: *"...for months, there wasn't a day that I didn't smoke. But no, not anymore. I was struck by the thought that, when I was in the throes of thinking, that I wouldn't do it anymore because it's an experience, like it's really bad. Because, for example, with my hypertension, one day I can, maybe I can smoke and the moment I fall asleep I won't be able to wake up."*

3.4 Theft

Most students who reported this behavior referred to minor shoplifting as isolated incidents, and when they were children. Motivations included stealing for fun, as a mischief, thoughtlessly, and due to peer influence or pressure. This behavior was also not reported at the private school. One student reported a failed attempt at home theft. Another mentioned hanging around with thieves in his neighborhood.

In the attempted robbery at a house, the student [SPS-E] said: *"...it didn't work, there were cameras, it was federal property, they caught me right there... I was with other friends, and they arrested us all."* Regarding the planning, he said: *"...it almost always starts beforehand, it's planned, and sometimes it just comes out in the moment, you know? ... sometimes they* [his friends] *also incite you... it's not that they pressure you, they incite you. If they tell you: 'well, do it!' it's like pressure, it's not like they're forcing you to do it, it's just that."*

Another student [NPS-A] said he had stolen small things and things from school: *"...well, things like, I don't know, things, like, I don't know, school materials or things like that, but not big things like that."*

3.5 Gang membership

Some students, including one girl, reported having belonged to or being part of a gang. Motivations ranged from a desire to be respected, fear of and following the gang leader, influence from friends and siblings, power and protection, fun and curiosity, and being invited. No gang membership was reported at the private school.

A student [SPS-D] referred to a gang in the neighborhood where she lives this way: *"Yes, it's the typical gang on my block, it's the Sureños 13* [name of the gang]*. So, yes, well, there's one of them here* [points to outside]*, he considers me a sureña. Yes,* [for him] *I am sureña 13...* [but] *I didn't want to join yet, because, well, to get into vices like them, well, no...* [but] *that gang really attracts my attention. I don't know, it's just the simple fact that, because there are a lot of gangs on my block, well, one is not so sure. Yes, if not and you are, for example, part of the Sureños 13, they have more respect for you because Sureños are the ones in charge."*

Another student [SPS-G] referring to gang membership said: *"Yes, well, it's that there, I don't know why, they say we're the most powerful in the neighborhood, in the part of the neighborhood where I live, they say we're the most intimidating. In other neighborhoods, I mean, everyone has their own thing, right? But when we go to Punta Oriente* [a neighborhood] *or something like that, well there we do have a place. Like there's a place called 'Banderas', a lot of gangs get together there, and so cholos* [young people from poor backgrounds who wear a particular outfit], *grupo* [urban youth] *and so on, well, we arrived too, right? Not so much causing a mess, but we arrive like that to play soccer or something. But we don't arrive violently, showing off or intimidating, right?"*

Another student [SPS-E] spoke about the protection and respect he receives from belonging to a gang: *"If you want to stop the recording and I can tell you, there's no problem* [the recording stops and mentions the name of the gang he belongs to, which he says is "wanted by the police"]; *"…I know that if something happens to me or if they want to do something to me, I have their support, just as they have mine, I also have to prove something to them, right? That they also have my support or show respect."* Regarding his entry into the gang, he said: *"…because of my brother, and my friends too, I started joining… since I was little, I was with my brother and he talked to me a lot about fights, since then I like fights a lot."* When asked about his feelings about being in a gang, he said: *"..yes, like a family, I see them as a family."*

3.6 Problems with the police

Four students reported having had difficulties with the police. They said they are sometimes mistaken for criminals, profiled based on their physical appearance, and stopped and searched because they are seen as suspicious. They consider this police abuse. Some students refer to the police with disrespect and insults. One student mentioned being caught stealing, another for getting into a fight with someone, and another says he lied to the police to avoid responsibility.

A student [SPS-E] said he had had problems for hitting another young man, which led to a restraining order: *"..yes, I have been in danger of being caught* [going to jail], *a serious crime, it's not like they caught me, and in the past they have filed charges against me, but they are just X* [unimportant], *the charges don't matter to me… they are charges that I can't get close to them and things like that, so for example for more serious crimes, but no, they haven't caught me."*

A student [SPS-G] spoke of the police officers when they came to interrogate them: *"The police are some disgusting, fat, damn men who were here and they arrived and then they came and asked the girls: 'Hey, are you being disturbed?'* [by her male friends] *…and things like we have damaged property?'… They ask for our parents or say that we do things that we shouldn't do or that we are in a place where we shouldn't be, I mean, very far from our home. That's why they wanted to take us* [into custody] *… they arrived imposing their authority, the bastards. They arrived and got off here, the fatties* [this is how he refers to the police officers]."

One student [STV-C] mentioned having been detained by the police with her male friends: *"…there were times when the police did come, but they didn't say anything to us… sometimes they asked us what we were doing and if it wasn't something, if we weren't carrying something bad. Then we would say no and that's it, they would leave. One time I was with some friends, and they looked, well, like… cholitos* [poor young people who wear a particular outfit], *like, like that, with tattoos and tacky clothing. Where I live, when they see someone like that, they stop to search them and they stopped me too because they thought I was carrying something, that if we didn't have drugs or weapons or anything… nothing, well they just asked if we had anything, they can't search me, and I told them no and that was it."*

3.7 Organized crime

Two students referred to drug traffickers. One of them mentioned that he met with drug traffickers, that he used and sold drugs, and that he also carried a gun. Another said that his relatives were involved in drug trafficking activities.

A student from the telesecundaria [STV-D] said: *"In Aldama* [a town nearby Chihuahua], *I used to meet up with some drug traffickers… he'd call me early to go with him and that's it... we'd go sell drugs, and there I tried it... I did use weapons, but not against a person; I used a gun."*

Another student [SPS-G] said: "*...when the police arrived, I wasn't scared because I have relatives who are police officers and so on. Aunts who are police officers, soldiers, and so on... and an uncle who's around, who's a drug dealer, too, right? He has a business across the street from my grandfather's house. And well, I'm not really afraid of them. I'm cautious but not scared.*"

3.8 Family problems

References to family difficulties were relatively frequent among the interviewed. Many students mentioned poor relationships, primarily with their father, mother, or stepfather and stepmother. They mentioned conflicts, arguments, and fights, as well as indifference and abandonment from their father or mother. Several mentioned living with grandparents. Some choose to distance themselves or isolate themselves to avoid the unhealthy family life and the discomfort it entails. Two students reported suicidal thoughts, and one mentioned cutting his skin as a way of letting off steam. Three students said their father was an alcoholic or a drug user, and one student said her father was in a rehabilitation center.

This is how a female student [STV-C] spoke about her relationship with her mother: "*Because I don't like to fight with her and I feel bad that sometimes she tells me things that I don't want to hear, so no, I try not to fight with her, but she does everything possible to fight with me... many times she tells me no, that I don't want to be with her, that I should go with my grandmother, that... ah!... that I wasn't a desired daughter, that I was like that, I don't know, things like that... we stop talking and each of us goes to our rooms.*"

Another student [SPS-E] referred to the distance from his mother; when asked why he decided not to live with his mother, he said: "*For the same reason, because of my stepfather.*" Now that he is older, when he is living with her, he says: "*...well, nothing, I lock myself in my room and don't go out until she arrives, or I leave. I felt bad about being with my mother because I did bad things and she worried about it, what a mother feels for her children, but in the end, I didn't want to come* [home with his mother] *but I felt bad and well, they try for you, and you don't value it. And I get along well with her, I like being here, but only with her* [not with the stepfather]."

A student [NTS-C] who reported sexting with her boyfriend and having access to a firearm belonging to her grandfather said: "*...in crazy moments like this, sometimes I want to go grab it and shoot myself.*" She also reported cutting herself: "*...before, I used to be a big fan of cutting myself, so I would grab them* [broken bottle glass] *and use them* [miming to cut her legs] *...it's because I have a lot of family problems and it eats me up inside... just on my legs, yes, on my arms it was mild because otherwise my mom would see them and well...*" When asked why and how often she cuts her body, she says with a broken voice: "*I don't know, I feel like I'm free, like it's my way of letting off steam... when? ... oh, I don't know, well, all the time, because I feel bad all the time, so...*".

Another student [SPS-G] referred to the abandonment of his father: "*...my biological father left when I was born and had children...I have a sister who is about 16 years old, that's all I know, I don't know my father or my sister...my brother is, right now that we're talking, my brother is about 9 years old, I think.*"

A student [SPS-B] talked about her difficult relationship with her mother: "*...she's always saying that I don't do anything, and I feel like I really only depend on my mother financially, nothing else... all of a sudden she's started kicking me out of the house... lately every fight, every weekend was just fighting and fighting and fighting, and I kind of hated* *her."* She then talked about her relationship with her mother: "*...when she starts saying that I'm really lazy and that she starts saying a lot of things, that I'm the one who's helped her the most or things like that, well it's because she depends on me more than I do on her... I don't need my mother to be okay, so to speak... a lot of times I do get angry, I try to calm down, but it's not always... or all of a sudden, I burst into tears, but it's very rare. And then it's like nothing happened. In fact, there came a time when I actually went to live with my sister, with one of my sisters.*"

Another student [SPS-E] referred to the abandonment of his parents when he was a baby: "*...there she is* [the mother], *she just left me when I was very little, I was still a baby, she left me with my grandparents and she went to other states and in other states she met a man and first she got married and then he died and she came back but she came back with two girls, twins... I see her from time to time, it's not like I have contact with her, I almost never see her, she came here recently to talk about some things about my father* [biological]*... I never knew him, but they came to tell me that he was gone...* [he died] *... and my grandfather who was like my father, he also died...*" When asked about how the death of his biological father affected him, he says: "*What about my father?* [his death] *I didn't care because I never knew him... I wanted to know him, but well, it's not like he did something to get to know me and then I don't care, they killed him, I think.*"

A student (NTS-E) reported having fights with his parents and sisters: "*...once I had a really bad fight with my dad and I said some really mean things to him. No, not nonsense, just really, really mean things, very insulting, very insulting.*" He then added: "*... my parents really do get on my nerves, and my sisters, that's why I almost always leave the house. And, in short, everything, all the problems, and everything I do is because of that. They blame me for a lot of things my sisters do, what other people do, and what's better for me. It's always, always the same. Then I tell them no, and they scold me for having answered them by saying no, and this, and that. And another problem, another conflict. They don't talk to me all day. I don't talk to them... I go and come home at night. I do my homework. They say something to me, and I respond well and fall asleep. But then that happens all over again the next day.*"

4. Discussion

This study was conducted to recognize the motivations behind criminal behaviors of adolescent students in the city of Chihuahua. The results showed that the problem is concentrated in at-risk groups; greater vulnerability was identified in schools located in poor and marginalized areas. The motivations that influence the occurrence of such behaviors should be considered when designing and implementing preventive action programs.

Carrying a gun was reported by several students, especially males, in low-income schools. According to a previously conducted survey of this population, having ever carried a gun had a prevalence of 7.4% [3]; this figure can be compared with US results for 2017–2019, where 6.3% of male and 2.4% of female students aged 14–15 carried a gun at least once in the previous year. The proportion was higher among those who experienced violence, suicidal ideation/attempt, or illicit substance use, which reflects the relevance of the phenomenon [15]. As to the motivation, the main reason given was for protection and security, especially among those living in dangerous and marginalized areas. Carrying a weapon was even encouraged by some parents. Bladed weapons such as knives or switchblades, which they reported taking secretly to school, were the most often mentioned with some even reported stabbing someone. However, there were also a couple of students who reported carrying firearms. The protection argument has been consistently referenced in the literature [16–21], although it has also been mentioned as a symbol of respect and power [16, 19, 21], and when making drug deals [19–21].

In Mexico, secondary school is the educational level where violence occurs most frequently, including physical violence [2]. In this sample of students, motivations for physical aggression included self-protection and defense of family or friends, to gain respect, impulsiveness or an aggressive personality, and as a reaction to insults or mistreatment. Bullying among peers was mentioned in several of the fights cited. Fights were reported as relatively frequent events, regardless of gender. Some men even cited encouragement from family members to learn how to fight. The topic of school violence has been widely addressed [22, 23], including in Mexico [2, 24, 25], which has led to numerous studies on preventive strategies and programs [26] that can be considered and adapted at the local level.

Substance use, which often begins in adolescence, is a significant contributor to the occurrence of various social pathologies such as violence, theft, and suicide [27]. In Mexico, as in other countries on the continent, alcohol and illicit drug use among junior high school students has been increasing [28], with prevalence rates close to those of students at the same school level in the United States [29]. For a decade now, the problem in the state of Chihuahua has been apparent as reflected in the higher percentage of "every drug" use among middle and high school students compared with the national average (19.8% vs. 11.1%; $p < 0.05$), as well as in the excessive use of alcohol (16.9%), and the ever-use of marijuana (11.9%), inhalants (5.1%), and cocaine (4.4%) [30]. In this study, the use of alcohol and drugs such as marijuana was reported by respondents from poor schools in the south, especially by men. However, the use of other substances such as methamphetamines, cocaine, inhalants, and psychotropic medications was also mentioned by some students. Most referred to perceived benefits. They cited positive sensations that help combat stress, depression, anxiety, and family problems. Few reported remorse for using or having used alcohol and/or drugs. Curiosity and peer pressure were also mentioned. In general, their use is hidden, especially from parents, either out of shame or fear of being exposed. Drug dealing in the neighborhoods they live in was mentioned, and some parents were even involved in this activity. The feeling of being in control over drug use was apparent, as if they could stop at any time. They know this is not accepted by their families and society, but they do not seem to be aware of the dependence caused or the physical and psychological consequences derived from their use. The existence of school interventions that promote students' academic engagement and that have an effect on reducing the use of alcohol and illicit drugs [31, 32] should be considered in this context.

The reported thefts were primarily from small convenience stores. Factors associated with theft in adolescents include cognitive and social impairments, academic failure, poor impulse control, personality disorders, family difficulties, substance use, and negative peer influences, among others [33–35]. The motivations mentioned in this study were mischief and peer influence or pressure. The most prominent thefts occurred among few male students from poor and marginalized schools. Recurrent gang thefts were prominent in two students, one of whom was apprehended. In Mexico, in 2022, robbery ranked second among the main crimes committed by adolescents, accounting for 19% of the total [36]. According to US statistics, nearly 10% of the population has reported having stolen at some point in their lives, with one in three people saying they started stealing before the age of 15 [35]. In Mexico, in 2022,

21% of the adolescent population within the comprehensive criminal justice system in Mexico reported that robbery was their first criminal act [36], which highlights the importance of taking preventive actions at an early age.

Gang membership was reported by four students from schools also located in the south of the city, including a woman. Gangs constitute a social problem that negatively affects the community's judicial, educational, and health systems [37]. Young people who join a gang are more likely to cause and receive violence, while the area in which they operate is also impacted by the resulting crime [38]. The desire to be respected, the search for prestige and protection, and the influence of friends or siblings were cited as primary motivations. The desire to belong, to feel part of something, was also mentioned. Membership was associated with activities such as stealing, fighting, and drug dealing. Although the proportion of students who belong to gangs in the local context is unknown, a representative study of high schools in the State of California reported that 8.4% of students considered themselves gang members [39], which gives an idea of the magnitude of the problem. Similar to the findings in this study, the main reason given for joining a gang is the need of protection, followed by fun, respect, money, or because a friend belongs to one [40]. It has also been observed that those who seek respect must commit a violent act against someone as an entry requirement [41], which adds to the need to prevent this social pathology. This issue can be addressed through community-based interventions that have proven successful [38].

Four students from marginalized schools reported difficulties with the police, including one arrested for committing crimes. It was mentioned with annoyance that they are profiled by the police for their physical appearance or for being away from home. Some students verbally referred to police officers in an offensive manner, in response to what they consider police arrogance. This points to the need to implement corrective measures in police conduct to prevent abuses of authority. These measures are reflected in the statistics of the comprehensive criminal justice system for adolescents in Mexico for 2022, where 45.9% of young people reported having suffered physical violence, 65.9% psychological violence, and 38.7% theft of money or looting of belongings during their arrest [36].

Two students from marginalized schools in the south reported being involved with drug traffickers and also mentioned family members being involved in drug trafficking. This was associated with carrying weapons and drug use. Although this phenomenon still seems localized and isolated in the study area, the fact that a direct relationship with drug traffickers was reported at an early age should be seen as a warning sign and a cause for concern given the vulnerability of these young people, especially those from low-income backgrounds who see it as an alternative to escape poverty [42, 43], and the lure of the world of narcoculture [44–46].

Family problems have been a determining and constant factor associated with risky behaviors among adolescents [47–49]. In this study, there were constant references to family dysfunction in almost all the students interviewed. Family disintegration was accompanied by difficulties maintaining healthy relationships between parents and children, especially with their parents' new husband or wife. Parental abandonment and disengagement from their children were a common narrative among several students. Some resorted to isolation to avoid problems, while others opted for direct conflicts with their parents. A couple of students reported self-destructive thoughts and behaviors, including suicidal thoughts. Addressing family problems is a major challenge, as interventions designed and implemented to treat young people with behavioral problems in developed countries do not seem to produce consistent benefits [50].

Antisocial and unlawful behavior in adolescents is a complex problem that requires a multifaceted and transdisciplinary approach. The relationship between these behaviors and psychological traits and disorders should not be underestimated. Through a combination of research, prevention, and intervention strategies, it is possible to reduce the incidence of these behaviors, facilitating healthier and more positive development for young people [51].

In the last decades, the study of antisocial and unlawful behavior in adolescents has gained great relevance in the fields of psychology, criminology, and other forensic sciences [52]. Studies on human behavior at this stage of life range from acts of disobedience, animal abuse, and rebellion to serious crimes such as kidnappings and femicides. These acts affect not only society but also the personal, emotional, and social development of the young people involved. Understanding the relationship between these behaviors and psychological traits and disorders is crucial for developing effective prevention and intervention strategies.

Personality traits such as a lack of empathy, low frustration tolerance, sensation-seeking, lack of guilt, or remorse are common in adolescents who exhibit antisocial behavior. These traits may be present and be indicators of disorders such as antisocial personality disorder and, in its extreme form, sociopathology or psychopathy.

Several factors contribute to the commission of unlawful and antisocial behavior in children and adolescents including family environment, particularly those environments characterized by a lack of supervision; abuse or neglect; and the presence of serious conflicts that can increase the likelihood of a teenager developing antisocial behavior; peer group with similar behaviors (school environment and friends play an important role in a teenager's propensity to engage in antisocial behavior) and psychological traits and disorders, including Attention Deficit Hyperactivity Disorder [53], Oppositional Defiant Disorder [54], Antisocial Personality Disorder, Conduct Disorder [55], and mood and anxiety disorders [56], have often been linked to antisocial and unlawful behaviors involving a difficult temperament in childhood, impulsivity, patterns of antisocial attitudes, and low empathy.

To address antisocial and unlawful behavior in adolescents, it is essential to implement prevention and intervention strategies that address both family and social factors, as well as individual psychological traits and disorders [57].

5. Conclusion

The crime problem appears to be concentrated in at-risk groups, especially in poor and marginalized areas, so efforts should be directed toward vulnerable students. The integrated results of the quantitative and qualitative phases provide relevant information for designing and implementing action programs aimed at preventing the motivators or triggers of criminal behavior in the identified high-risk groups.

There are various preventive strategies that should be considered to tackle this problem. For instance, parent training programs, family therapy, and support in so-called "positive parenting" can help improve the family environment; mentoring programs, extracurricular activities, and strengthening social cohesion can also reduce the negative influence of peers [58]. Early detection of problematic traits and behaviors at early stages is essential [59].

Acknowledgements

The authors wish to thank students and school authorities for their participation. This study was funded by the Chihuahua Business Foundation (FECHAC: Fundación del Empresariado Chihuahuense Asociación Civil) and University Claustro of Chihuahua.

Conflict of interest

The authors declare no conflict of interest.

Author details

Joel Monárrez-Espino[1,2*], Luisa Villareal-Varela[1], Estefanía Pinzón-Kranz[3], Lorena Ávila-Carrasco[2], Margarita Martínez-Fierro[2] and Jesús Vaca-Cortés[1]

1 Research Department, University Claustro of Chihuahua, Mexico

2 Unit of Medicine and Health Sciences, Autonomous University of Zacatecas, Mexico

3 Institute of Social and Cultural Anthropology, Free University of Berlin, Germany

*Address all correspondence to: joel.monarrez@claustro.edu.mx

References

[1] Azaola E. Diagnóstico de las y los adolescentes que cometen delitos graves en México. Fondo de las Naciones Unidas para la Infancia. 2015. Available from: https://www.casede.org/BibliotecaCasede/Diagnostico_adolescentes.pdf

[2] Comisión Nacional para la Mejora Continua de la Educación. La violencia entre estudiantes de educación básica y media superior en México. Aportaciones sobre u frecuencia y variables asociadas a partir de estudios de gran escala. Informe Ejecutivo, Editorial Mejoredu, México. 2021. Available from: https://www.mejoredu.gob.mx/images/publicaciones/informe-ejecutivo-violencia.pdf

[3] Monárrez-Espino J, León-Ramírez CL, Vázquez-Ríos ME, Montes-Meléndez D, Ávila-Carrasco L, Martínez-Fierro M, et al. Antisocial and criminal behaviors of secondary school students from the city of Chihuahua in Northern Mexico and associated risk factors. Acción Psicológica. 2022;**19**:95-110. DOI: 10.5944/ap.19.1.34431

[4] Silverman D. Doing Qualitative Research. California, US: Sage Publications. Thousand Oaks; 2003

[5] Cook K. Using critical ethnography to explore issues in health promotion. Qualitative Health Research. 2005;**15**:129-138. DOI: 10.1177/1049732304267751

[6] Seisdedos-Cubero N. Cuestionario A-D: Conductas Antisociales-Delictivas. Madrid, España: TEA Ediciones; 1995. Available from: https://es.scribd.com/document/716713005/Cuestioario-de-Conductucas-Antisociales-y-Delicitivas-a-D

[7] Seisdedos-Cubero N, Sánchez-Escobedo P. Cuestionario de conductas antisociales-delictivas A-D. México: Manual Moderno; 2001

[8] Gaeta ML, Galvanovskis A. Propensión a conductas antisociales y delictivas en adolescentes mexicanos. Psicología Iberoamericana. 2011;**19**: 47-54. DOI: 10.48102/pi.v19i2.229

[9] Sánchez-Velasco A, Galicia-Moyeda IX, Robles-Ojeda FJ. Conductas antisociales y delictivas en adolescentes: relación con el género, la estructura familiar y el rendimiento académico. Alternativas en Psicología. 2018;**38**:80-98. Available from: https://www.alternativas.me/attachments/article/158/6%20-%20Conductas%20antisociales-delictivas%20en%20adolescentes.pdf

[10] Murphy E, Dingwall R. The ethics of ethnography. In: Atkinson P, Coffey A, Delamont S, Lofland L, Lofland J, editors. Handbook of Ethnography. London, UK: Sage Publications; 2001. pp. 339-351

[11] Seidman I. Interviewing as Qualitative Research: A Guide for Researchers in Education and the Social Sciences. New York, US: Teachers College Press; 2013

[12] Morris A. A Practical Introduction to In-Depth Interviewing. California, US: SAGE Publications. Thousand Oaks; 2015. DOI: 10.4135/9781473921344

[13] Emerson RM, Fretz RI, Shaw LL. Writing Ethnographic Fieldnotes. US: University of Chicago Press; 1995

[14] Hsieh HF, Shannon SE. Three approaches to qualitative content analysis. Qualitative Health

Research. 2005;**15**:1277-1288. DOI: 10.1177/1049732305276687

[15] Simon TR, Clayton HB, Dahlberg LL, David-Ferdon C, Kilmer G, Barbero C. Gun carrying among youths, by demographic characteristics, associated violence experiences, and risk behaviors - United States, 2017-2019. Morbidity and Mortality Weekly Report. 2022;**71**:953-957. DOI: 10.15585/mmwr.mm7130a1

[16] Ash P, Kellermann AL, Fuqua-Whitley D, Johnson A. Gun Acquisition and use by juvenile offenders. Journal of the American Medical Association. 1996;**275**:1754-1758. DOI: 10.1001/jama.1996.03530460058032

[17] Wilkinson DL, Fagan J. The role of firearms in violence 'scripts': The dynamics of gun events among adolescent males. Law and Contemporary Problems. 1996;**59**:55-59. DOI: 10.2307/1192210

[18] Freed LH, Webster DW, Longwell JJ, Carrese J, Wilson MH. Factors preventing gun acquisition and carrying among incarcerated adolescent males. Archives of Pediatrics and Adolescent Medicine. 2021;**155**:335-341. DOI: 10.1001/archpedi.155.3.335

[19] Black S, Hausman A. Adolescents' views of guns in a high-violence community. Journal of Adolescent Research. 2008;**23**:592-610. DOI: 10.1177/0743558408322142

[20] Wilkinson DL, McBryde MS, Williams B, Bloom S, Bell K. Peers and gun use among urban adolescent males: An examination of social embeddedness. Journal of Contemporary Criminal Justice. 2009;**25**:20-44. DOI: 10.1177/10439862083

[21] Oliphant SN, Mouch CA, Rowhani-Rahbar A, Hargarten S, Jay J, Hemenway D, et al. A scoping review of patterns, motives, and risk and protective factors for adolescent firearm carriage. Journal of Behavioral Medicine. 2019;**42**:763-810. DOI: 10.1007/s10865-019-00048-x

[22] King M. The Crisis of School Violence. A New Perspective. US: Michigan State University Press; 2020

[23] Turanovic JJ, Siennick SE. The Causes and Consequences of School Violence. USA: A Review. National Institute of Justice; 2022. Available from: https://files.eric.ed.gov/fulltext/ED619329.pdf

[24] Saucedo-Ramos CL, Guzmán-Gómez C. La investigación sobre la violencia escolar en México: tendencias, tensiones y desafíos. Revista Cultura y Representaciones Sociales. 2018;**24**:213-245. DOI: 10.28965/2018-024-08

[25] Tronco-Paganelli J, Madrigal-Ramírez A. Violencia escolar en México: una exploración en sus dimensiones y consecuencias. Trabajo Social UNAM. 2016;**4**:9-27. DOI: 10.22201/ents.20075987p.2013.4.54048

[26] Lester S, Lawrence C, Ward C. What do we know about preventing school violence? A systematic review of systematic reviews. Psychology Health and Medicine. 2017;**22**:187-233. DOI: 10.1080/13548506.2017.1282616

[27] United Nations Office on Drugs and Crime. World Drug Report. UNODC Research; 2023. Available from: https://www.unodc.org/unodc/en/data-and-analysis/world-drug-report-2023.html

[28] Inter-American Drug Abuse Control Commission. Report on Drug Use in the Americas 2019. Washington, US: Editorial Organization of American States; 2019

[29] Miech RA, Johnston LD, Patrick ME, O'Malley PM, Bachman JG, Schulenberg JE. Monitoring the Future. National Survey Results on Drug Use, 1975-2022: Secondary School Students. Monitoring the Future Monograph Series. Institute for Social Research, University of Michigan, US; 2022. Available from: https://monitoringthefuture.org/wp-content/uploads/2022/12/mtf2022.pdf

[30] Villatoro-Velázquez JA, Medina-Mora IME, del Campo-Sánchez RM, Fregoso-Ito DA, Bustos-Gamiño MN, Resendiz-Escobar E, et al. El consumo de drogas en estudiantes de México: tendencias y magnitud del problema. Salud Mental. 2016;**39**:193-203. DOI: 10.17711/SM.0185-3325.2016.023

[31] Christie GIG, Cheetham A, Lubman DI. Interventions for alcohol and drug use disorders in young people: 10 key evidence-based approaches to inform service delivery. Current Addiction Reports. 2020;**7**:464-474. DOI: 10.1007/s40429-020-00336-6

[32] Melendez-Torres GJ, Ponsford R, Falconer J, Bonell C. Whole-school interventions promoting student commitment to school to prevent substance use and violence: A systematic review. Public Health. 2023;**221**:190-197. DOI: 10.1016/j.puhe.2023.06.021

[33] Greening L. Adolescent stealers' and nonstealers' social problem-solving skills. Adolescence. 1997;**32**:51-55

[34] Moncher FJ, Miller GE. Nondelinquent youths' stealing behavior and their perceptions of parents, school, and peers. Adolescence. 1999;**34**:577-591

[35] Blanco C, Grant J, Petry NM, Simpson HB, Alegria A, Liu SM, et al. Prevalence and correlates of shoplifting in the United States: Results from the National Epidemiologic Survey on alcohol and related conditions (NESARC). American Journal of Psychiatry. 2008;**165**:905-913. DOI: 10.1176/appi.ajp.2008.07101660

[36] Instituto Nacional de Estadística Geografía. Encuesta Nacional de Adolescentes en el Sistema de Justicia Penal. INEGI, México. 2023. Available from: www.inegi.org.mx/contenidos/saladeprensa/boletines/2023/ENASJUP/ENASJUP2022.pdf

[37] Simon TR, Ritter NM, Mahendra RR. Changing course. Preventing Gang Membership. US: National Institute of Justice - National Center of Injury Prevention and Control; 2014. Available from: https://www.ojp.gov/pdffiles1/nij/239234.pdf

[38] Howell JC. Why is gang-membership prevention important? In: Simon TR, Ritter NM, Mahendra RR, editors. Changing Course. Preventing Gang Membership. US: National Institute of Justice - National Center of Injury Prevention and Control; 2014. pp. 7-18. Available from: https://www.ojp.gov/pdffiles1/nij/239234.pdf

[39] Nuñez-Estrada J, Gilreath TD, Astor RA, Benbenishty R. A statewide study of gang membership in California secondary schools. Youth and Society. 2016;**48**:720-736. DOI: 10.1177/0044118X14528957

[40] Taylor CS, Smith PR. The attraction of gangs: How can we reduce it? In: Simon TR, Ritter NM, Mahendra RR, editors. Changing Course. Preventing Gang Membership. US: National Institute of Justice - National Center of Injury Prevention and Control; 2014. pp. 19-30. Available from: https://www.ojp.gov/pdffiles1/nij/239234.pdf

[41] Descormiers K, Corrado RR. The right to belong: Individual motives and youth gang initiation rites. Deviant Behavior. 2016;**36**:1341-1359. DOI: 10.1080/01639625.2016.1177390

[42] Emmerich R. Estudios sobre el narcotráfico en América Latina. Argentina: Infancia y narcotráfico en México. Universidad de Belgrano; 2014. Available from: http://repositorio.ub.edu.ar/bitstream/handle/123456789/2627/300_Emmerich.pdf?sequence=1&isAllowed=y

[43] Almanza-Avendaño AM, Gómez-San Luis AH, Guzmán-González DN, Cruz-Montes JA. Representaciones sociales acerca del narcotráfico en adolescentes de Tamaulipas. Región y Sociedad. 2018;**30**:a286. DOI: 10.22198/rys.2018.72.a846

[44] Baca-Zapata G. Aproximación a la narcocultura como referente de la construcción identitaria de jóvenes en México. El Cotidiano. 2017;**206**:59-87. Available from: https://www.redalyc.org/pdf/325/32553518007.pdf

[45] Becerra-Romero AT. Investigación documental sobre la narcocultura como objeto de estudio en México. Culturales. 2018;**6**:e349. DOI: 10.22234/recu.20180601.e349

[46] Becerra-Romero AR, Hernández-Cruz DA. Fascinación por el poder: consumo y apropiación de la narcocultura por jóvenes en contextos de narcotráfico. Instersticios Sociales. 2019;**17**:259-285. DOI: 10.55555/IS.17.235

[47] Ingram KM, Espelage DL, Davis JP, Merrin GJ. Family violence, sibling, and peer aggression during adolescence: Associations with behavioral health outcomes. Frontiers in Psychiatry. 2020;**11**:26. DOI: 10.3389/fpsyt.2020.00026

[48] Bozzini AB, Bauer A, Maruyama J, Simoes R, Matijasevich A. Factors associated with risk behaviors in adolescence: A systematic review. Brazilian Journal of Psychiatry. 2021;**43**:210-221. DOI: 10.1590/1516-4446-2019-0835

[49] Silva GRE, Lima MLC, Acioli RML, Barreira AK. A influência da violência familiar e entre pares na prática do bullying por adolescentes escolares. Ciência e Saúde Coletiva. 2021;**26**:4933-4943. DOI: 10.1590/1413-812320212611.3.20632019

[50] Littell JH, Pigott TD, Nilsen KH, Roberts J, Labrum TK. Functional family therapy for families of youth (age 11-18) with behaviour problems: A systematic review and meta-analysis. Campbell Systematic Reviews. 2023;**19**:e1324. DOI: 10.1002/cl2.1324

[51] Vaca-Cortés J, Dzib P. La máscara del asesino. México: Ediciones de la Universidad Autónoma de Yucatán; 2018

[52] Romero E, Luengo MA, Gómez-Fraguela JA. Factores psicosociales y delincuencia: Un estudio de efectos recíprocos. Escritos de Psicología. 2000;**4**:78-91

[53] Diez-Zamorano M, López-Villalobos AJ, Serrano-Pintado I, Vicente GL. Relación entre el tipo de apego y los eventos traumáticos vividos en adolescentes en riesgo psicosocial, en función del criterio tener o no tener Trastorno por Déficit de Atención e Hiperactividad (TDAH). Revista Iberoamericana de Psicología. 2023;**16**:101-121. DOI: 10.33881/2027-1786.rip.16210

[54] Palacio-Ortiz J, Peña-Quintero C, Gómez-Valero M, Bustamante-Gómez P, Arroyave-Sierra P, Vargas-Upeguí C, et al. Trastornos psiquiátricos a través

de la vida: un estudio de comparación de hijos de padres con trastorno afectivo bipolar tipo I frente a hijos de padres controles de la comunidad. Revista Colombiana de Psiquiatria. 2017;**46**: 129-139. DOI: 10.1016/j.rcp.2016.06.007

[55] Fruto-López YA, Ferrás-Mosquera LM, Toranzo-Castro N. Estrategia pedagógica para la formación del psicopedagogo en la atención a trastorno de conducta. Didáctica y Educación. 2024;**5**:213-228

[56] García-Vázquez P. Estabilidad Diagnóstica Del Trastorno Bipolar. Una Revisión Sistemática. Acción Psicológica. 2022;**19**:71-84. DOI: 10.5944/ap.19.1.33690Gorsuch

[57] Romero E, Luengo MA, Gómez-Fraguela JA, Sobral J. The structure of personality traits in adolescents: The five-factor model and the alternative five. Psicothema. 2002;**14**:134-143

[58] Caballero LM, Giner-Alegría CA. Política Criminal en Menores Infractores. Prevención De Conductas Delictivas en España Tomando Como Referencia Las Directrices De Las Naciones Unidas. Revista Vox Juris. 2023;**1**:105-114. DOI: 10.24265/voxjuris.2023.v41n2.09

[59] Gutiérrez-Vaca NR. Infantes y adolescentes en conflicto con la ley penal en México. Archivos de Criminología, Criminalística y Seguridad Privada. 2023;**1**:168-178

Chapter 3

From Insight to Intervention: The Evolving Landscape of Personality Disorders

Akanksha Shankar and Shubham Sharma

Abstract

Personality disorders (PDs) represent complex, enduring patterns of cognition, emotion, and behaviour that significantly impair functioning and quality of life. This chapter explores recent advances in the understanding, diagnosis, and treatment of PDs, highlighting a paradigm shift from traditional categorical models toward dimensional and trait-based frameworks exemplified by the DSM-5 Alternative Model for Personality Disorders (AMPD) and ICD-11. We review emerging insights into the aetiology and neurobiology of PDs, emphasising the interplay of genetic, developmental, and psychosocial factors. Advances in assessment methodologies, including digital tools and cross-cultural considerations, are discussed alongside persistent challenges such as stigma, misdiagnosis, and treatment resistance. Evidence-based psychotherapies—Dialectical Behaviour Therapy, Mentalisation-Based Treatment, Transference-Focused Psychotherapy, Schema Therapy, and Cognitive Behavioural Therapy—are evaluated in terms of effectiveness and mechanisms of change. The chapter concludes by examining future directions involving digital health innovations, machine learning, neuroimaging, and early intervention strategies, underscoring the promise of personalised psychiatry. By integrating evolving research into clinical practice, this chapter aims to foster nuanced, evidence-informed approaches that enhance outcomes and reduce the burden of personality disorders.

Keywords: personality disorder, borderline personality disorders, psychotherapy, personalised psychiatry, early intervention

1. Introduction

Personality disorders (PD) involves a persistent pattern of inner experience and conduct that significantly deviates from societal norms and expectations [1, 2]. In psychiatric diagnosis and clinical practice, PDs have typically had a dubious position due to their long-standing perception as inflexible, challenging to treat, and not very well understood. The way these mental health conditions are conceived of, evaluated, and treated has changed significantly in recent decades, due to advancements in neuroscience, dimensional models of personality, and evidence-based treatments.

The limits of conventional categorisation frameworks, such as those described in the DSM-IV and ICD-10, are becoming more widely acknowledged in the field. The ICD-11 dimensional model and the DSM-5 Alternative Model for Personality Disorders (AMPD) have arisen in response, with a focus on maladaptive personality traits and deficits in interpersonal and self-function as key diagnostic constructs [3, 4]. Converging data from developmental, neurocognitive, and genetic studies support these changes by underlining the spectrum traits of pathology of personality and how it interacts with psychosocial and environmental risk factors. Treatment research has advanced significantly in tandem with these changes in diagnosis. The effectiveness of evidence-based treatments, such as mentalisation-based treatment (MBT), transference-focused psychotherapy (TFP), dialectical behaviour therapy (DBT), and schema therapy, has been shown, especially for borderline personality disorder [5]. Greater adaptability and individualisation in clinical care have also been rendered possible by the increasing recognition of transdiagnostic and modular therapy techniques. This chapter discusses the changing field of personality disorders, encompassing fundamental understandings of aetiology and classification, to the most recent advancements in therapeutic intervention.

2. Shifting paradigms: From categorical to dimensional models

For many years, PDs were defined using a categorical structure in the DSM-IV and ICD-10. Although this approach offered uniform nomenclature and therapeutic benefit, it has drawn a lot of criticism for a number of conceptual and methodological shortcomings. The diagnostic criteria characteristics were frequently shared by other personality disorders, making it challenging to identify the specific type of PD. For instance, there were several notable parallels between histrionic and borderline personality disorders. Individuals with the same diagnosis of PD may exhibit diverse symptom patterns affecting accuracy and diagnostic credibility [6]. Longitudinal studies demonstrate significant symptom variability, which challenges and contradicts the notion that PDs are stable over time. The prevalence of cross-cultural variations makes it challenging to meet the diagnostic criteria worldwide.

DSM-5 (2013) and the ICD-11 (2022) implemented dimensional approaches to personality disorder classification, which caused a significant change in how psychopathology is defined [7].

2.1 DSM-5 alternative model for personality disorders (AMPD)

The AMPD presented a distinctive and research-based paradigm. It is made up of two major elements:

1. Criteria A: Personality Functioning Level: focuses on deficiencies in interpersonal (empathy, intimacy) and self-functioning (identification, self-direction)

2. Criterion B: Pathological Personality Traits: Negative affectivity, detachment, antagonism, disinhibition, and psychoticism are five general trait categories that correspond to aspects of the Five-Factor Model of personality [3, 8, 9].

This continuous, multilevel, hierarchical model offers a more comprehensive clinical picture and is more consistent with personality studies.

2.2 ICD-11-dimensional model

The categorical PD framework was replaced by an integrated dimensional model that focuses on

1. Severity of personality dysfunction: Mild, moderate, or severe based on global functional impairments

2. Trait domain qualifiers: Similar to the DSM-5 AMPD, ICD-11 includes trait domains such as negative affectivity, detachment, dis-sociality, disinhibition, and anankastic.

This paradigm improves diagnostic variability and clinical relevance across cultures by enabling both the dominant characteristic manifestations and the degree of impairment.

3. Aetiology and pathophysiology: What drives personality disorders?

Personality disorders (PDs) have an intricate aetiology that includes interactions between environmental factors, neurological abnormalities, and genetic predispositions. Together, these elements influence persistent thought, emotion, and behaviour patterns that characterise disordered personality functioning.

3.1 Genetic factors

According to twin and family studies, 30–60% of the variation in personality traits and susceptibility to PDs can be attributed to hereditary factors. According to Livesley et al., heritability estimates are especially high for Cluster B disorders, such as borderline and antisocial [10]. Temperamental qualities such as impulsivity, negative affectivity, and emotional instability can predispose people to personality pathology under specific circumstances, although genetic variables may not directly cause PDs [11].

3.2 Neurobiological factors

Developments in neurophysiology and neuroimaging have shown that people with PD exhibit structural and functional changes in their brains, especially in regions linked to impulse control, emotion management, and social cognition (**Figure 1**).

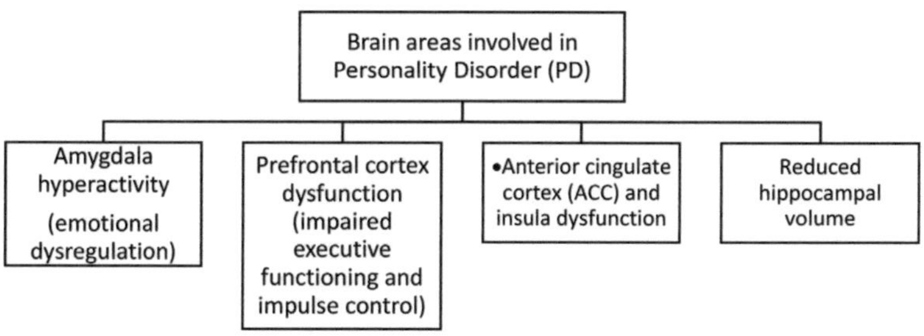

Figure 1.
Brain areas involved in PD.

3.3 Environmental contributions

The course of development of PDs is significantly influenced by environmental adversity, especially in the development of aberrant relationship patterns and issues with emotion regulation. The key contributors are:

- Childhood maltreatment and trauma (physical, sexual, or emotional)
- Parental neglect
- Disruptions to attachment (e.g., early loss, maternal separation)
- Stress and socioeconomic insecurity

Environmental risk factors are not deterministic; rather, they interact with genetic vulnerabilities *via* gene-environment interplay (e.g., through epigenetic pathways) to influence brain development and personality formation.

3.4 Early developmental risk factors

Early life experiences are the developmental origins of many personality disorders, particularly during crucial stages of social learning and identity formation. Childhood attachment styles that are disorganised or insecure are associated with a higher risk of borderline personality disorder (BPD) and other PDs. Early risk factors for maladaptive personality traits include increased reactivity, behavioural inhibition, or a lack of deliberate control. During early family settings, maladaptive coping mechanisms may be modelled or reinforced, leading to long-lasting problematic interpersonal patterns. Affect regulation, interpersonal functioning, and self-concept are all major impairments across PDs, and these early disturbances impede their normal development [12].

3.5 Characteristics vs. disorder

Differentiating between pathological and normal personality variance is a major topic of discussion in the study of personality disorders. According to the dimensional trait paradigm, PDs are not qualitatively different situations, but rather severe or maladaptive variations of normal features. For instance, conscientiousness can border on obsessive-compulsive tendencies when excessive, while introversion can exist on a continuum with detachment. According to Krueger and Markon, pathology is defined by the inflexibility, pervasiveness, and detrimental effects on functioning of features rather than just their presence [13]. Understanding how brain structures interact with emotional processing, attachment, and interpersonal dynamics offers crucial insight into both the pathogenesis and treatment of PDs.

3.6 Emotion regulation and impulse control

Dysregulation of affect and behaviour is a key neuropsychological feature of many PDs, including BPD and antisocial PD. Increased emotional reactivity, trouble regaining equilibrium following emotional stimulation, and a dependence on unhealthy coping strategies (such as aggressiveness or self-harm) are all signs of emotion dysregulation. Dysfunctions in the serotonergic and dopaminergic systems, especially in the prefrontal-limbic circuits, are often the cause of deficiencies in impulse control.

A common cause of impulsive behaviour is the inability to control emotional reactions prior to acting [14].

These deficits are especially addressed by emerging therapies such as mentalisation-based therapy (MBT) and dialectical behaviour therapy (DBT), which improve reflective functioning, emotional awareness, and distress tolerance.

3.7 Attachment theory and interpersonal dysfunction

A crucial psychosocial foundation for comprehending the interpersonal challenges that define personality disorders is provided by attachment theory. Early encounters with carers create internal conceptualisations of oneself and other people that serve as the foundation for interpersonal behaviour and last throughout adulthood.

The development of PD is intimately linked to insecure or disordered attachment:

- Disorganised or anxious-preoccupied attachment, which is characterised by a fear of abandonment and erratic interpersonal connections, is closely associated with borderline PD.
- People with schizoid or narcissistic traits are more likely to exhibit avoidant or dismissive attachment styles, which frequently result in emotional detachment and a lack of empathy.

4. Evidence-based treatments: What works and why

Over the past three decades, advances in psychotherapy research have significantly improved the treatment landscape for personality disorders (PDs), particularly borderline personality disorder (BPD). Once considered untreatable, PDs are now viewed as modifiable conditions, responsive to structured, evidence-based interventions. Among these, several therapies have gained empirical support and are increasingly personalised to fit patient profiles and treatment contexts.

4.1 Overview of psychotherapies

The most well-known psychotherapies for personality disorders, including BPD, all include a relational, integrative, and organised approach [5]. An overview of the most well-known evidence-based models may be found below:

4.1.1 Dialectical behaviour therapy (DBT)

DBT, which was originated by Marsha Linehan in 1993, combines dialectical theory, mindfulness, and cognitive-behavioural concepts. People with emotional dysregulation, persistent suicidality, and self-harming behaviours benefit most from it.

- Fundamental modules: mindfulness, interpersonal effectiveness, distress tolerance, and emotion management.
- Evidence: According to Linehan et al., a number of randomised controlled trials (RCTs) show increased emotional stability, fewer psychiatric hospitalisations, and decreased self-harm.

4.1.2 Mentalisation-based therapy (MBT)

Based on attachment theory, MBT was created by Fonagy and Bateman to address mentalising impairments, or the inability to comprehend one's own and other people's mental states.

Enhancing emotional intelligence and thoughtful functioning in social situations is the main goal.

- Evidence: Long-term research demonstrates consistent declines in interpersonal dysfunction, suicidality, and BPD symptoms [15].

4.1.3 Transference-focused psychotherapy (TFP)

It has its roots in object relations theory, places a strong emphasis on the therapeutic alliance as a setting for comprehending and reorganising fragmented internal representations of oneself and other people.

- Focus: Integrating fractured self-structures by elucidating and comprehending transference patterns.

- Evidence: Studies reveal gains in controlling impulses, relationships. Quality, and incorporating identities [16].

4.1.4 Schema therapy

Schema therapy was created by Jeffrey Young and uses cognitive, behavioural, and experiential methods to treat early maladaptive schemas, which are ingrained patterns that were formed during childhood.

- The main goals are to modify unhealthy coping mechanisms and reparent the "vulnerable child" mentality.

- Evidence: Proven to be beneficial for BPD as well as narcissistic, dependent, and avoidant PDs; several trials have shown long-term effects.

4.1.5 Cognitive behavioural therapy (CBT)

The goal of CBT for PDs is to recognise and change dysfunctional attitudes and actions. Cluster C (anxious-avoidant) personality disorders are the most common conditions for which it is utilised.

Restructuring unhelpful ideas and actions is the main goal.

- Evidence: CBT has demonstrated a moderate level of effectiveness, particularly in lowering reliance and avoidance.

4.1.6 Treatment outcome data and effectiveness

Systematic and manualised psychotherapies can considerably improve PD symptomatology according to various research studies. Significant decreases in self-harm, suicidality, and hospitalisation are linked to DBT, MBT, TFP, and structured therapy.

DOI: http://dx.doi.org/10.5772/intechopen.1012272

MBT and TFP show improvements in interpersonal functioning and emotional regulation, along with long-lasting symptom improvements after treatment. CBT-based therapies are beneficial for Cluster C illnesses and are increasingly being modified for other clusters through integration with schema or mindfulness techniques. Schema therapy has demonstrated broad-spectrum effectiveness across various PD forms.

Although most therapies have moderate effect sizes and are most effective when tailored to the disease, motivation, and developmental history of the individual. Meta-analyses support the idea that specialised treatments are better than treatments as usual.

4.2 Mechanisms of change and treatment personalisation

Customising therapies for each patient requires an understanding of these treatments' mechanisms of change. Typical therapy approaches consist of:

- Better mentalisation and interpersonal insight (MBT)
- Better emotion regulation (DBT, MBT)
- Combining fragmented representations of the self and the object (TFP)
- Altering fundamental belief systems and schemas (Schema therapy)
- Cognitive restructuring and behavioural activation (CBT)

4.2.1 Challenges and controversies in personality disorder research and treatment

Even though there have been significant advancements in the understanding and management of personality disorders (PDs), a number of persistent issues and disputes restrict the best possible clinical care and impede the advancement of research. These include ongoing stigma, inaccurate diagnoses, treatment resistance in complicated situations, and moral conundrums related to ongoing labelling and action.

4.2.2 Treatment-resistant cases

Treatment resistance is still a significant therapeutic problem, particularly in severe, chronic, or concomitant cases, even though many PDs are now thought to be curable.

Treatment resistance is linked to the following factors:

- Profound dissociation or a history of trauma
- Co-occurring substance abuse or signs of psychosis
- A weak therapeutic alliance or a high dropout rate
- Inadequate reflective thinking, drives, or understanding

Treatment resistance may be a result of insufficient treatment duration, inconsistencies between diagnosis and intervention, or limits of the existing therapy model rather than being a failure of the patient or therapist. For complicated presentations, long-term or integrative approaches—like integrating DBT or MBT with schema therapy—are being investigated more and more.

Research also emphasises the necessity of:

- Improved early detection of high-risk individuals, such as teenagers exhibiting nascent characteristics
- Treatment models with tiers according to severity
- Creation of modular therapies based on the functional limitations and trait profile of the individual.

5. Future directions in research and clinical practice

The way that doctors think about, identify, and treat personality disorders (PDs) is changing as a result of new technologies, innovative assessment techniques, and individualised methods. Interdisciplinary research, early preventative initiatives, and the increasing potential of personalised psychiatry are likely to propel future advancements [17].

6. Prevention strategies and early intervention

There are chances for prevention and early intervention, as it is becoming more well acknowledged that PDs frequently have developmental antecedents in infancy and adolescence.

- Screening adolescents with emotional and behavioural dysregulation, peer difficulties, or early trauma may help identify youth at risk for developing PDs.
- Evidence-based programmes such as emotion coaching, parent-child interaction therapy, and school-based interventions can reduce the likelihood of persistent dysfunction into adulthood [18].
- Early-stage interventions (e.g., MBT-A, DBT for adolescents) have demonstrated effectiveness in reducing self-harm and improving interpersonal functioning in youth with emerging BPD traits.
- The emphasis on tiered treatment and preventive mental health in this early intervention strategy is consistent with larger psychiatric trends.

7. The promise of personalised psychiatry

Precision and personalisation, or tailoring therapy to each patient's unique biological, psychological, and social characteristics, are key to the future of PD treatment.

- Using dimensional models (such as the DSM-5 AMPD and ICD-11) to inform therapy selection, trait-based and severity-informed treatment planning is one of the main developments.

- Biomarker-informed psychiatry, in which personalised risk assessment and therapy are guided by genetic, neurological, or digital phenotypes.

- Adaptive and modular therapies that adjust particular elements (such as trauma processing, emotion management, and interpersonal skills) to the patient's need, drive, and ability to change.

8. Conclusion

With advances in the neurobiological, diagnostic, and therapeutic domains, personality disorders are no longer viewed as being difficult to cure. This chapter aids in comprehending this novel conceptual development that will be beneficial for future clinical applications and treatment.

9. Summary of key takeaways

1. Paradigm shift in diagnosis: The field is moving from rigid categorical models (e.g., DSM-IV, ICD-10) to dimensional and trait-based frameworks (e.g., DSM-5 AMPD, ICD-11), which better capture the complexity and spectrum of personality pathology.

2. Aetiology and neurobiology: PDs arise from an interplay of genetic predispositions, early developmental adversity, neurobiological dysfunction, and interpersonal experiences—highlighting the need for integrative, biopsychosocial models.

3. Evidence-based treatments: Psychotherapies such as DBT, MBT, TFP, schema therapy, and CBT have demonstrated significant efficacy, particularly for BPD. Mechanisms of change include improved emotion regulation, mentalisation, and restructuring of maladaptive schemas.

Acknowledgements

The author acknowledges the use of QuillBot for language polishing of the manuscript.

Author details

Akanksha Shankar* and Shubham Sharma
King George's Medical University, Lucknow, Uttar Pradesh, India

*Address all correspondence to: akks1420@gmail.com

References

[1] American Psychiatric Association. Diagnostic and Statistical Manual of Mental Disorders: DSM-5™. 5th ed. Vol. xliv. Arlington, VA, USA: American Psychiatric Publishing, Inc.; 2013. 947 p

[2] WHO Releases 2025 Update to the International Classification of Diseases (ICD-11) [Internet]. Available from: https://www.who.int/news/item/14-02-2025-who-releases-2025-update-to-the-international-classification-of-diseases-(icd-11) [Accessed: July 14, 2025]

[3] Krueger RF, Hobbs KA. An overview of the DSM-5 alternative model of personality disorders. Psychopathology. 2020;**53**(3-4):126-132

[4] Hopwood CJ, Kotov R, Krueger RF, Watson D, Widiger TA, Althoff RR, et al. The time has come for dimensional personality disorder diagnosis. Personality and Mental Health. 2018;**12**(1):82-86

[5] Psychological Therapies for People With Borderline Personality Disorder - PubMed [Internet]. Available from: https://pubmed.ncbi.nlm.nih.gov/32368793/ [Accessed: July 14, 2025]

[6] Tyrer P, Reed GM, Crawford MJ. Classification, Assessment, Prevalence, and Effect of Personality Disorder. Available from: https://www.thelancet.com/journals/lancet/article/PIIS0140-6736(14)61995-4/abstract [Accessed: July 14, 2025]

[7] Bach B, Markon K, Simonsen E, Krueger RF. Clinical utility of the DSM-5 alternative model of personality disorders: Six cases from practice. Journal of Psychiatric Practice. 2015;**21**(1):3-25

[8] Miller JD, Sleep C, Lynam DR. DSM-5 alternative model of personality disorder: Testing the trait perspective captured in criterion B. Current Opinion in Psychology. 2018;**21**:50-54

[9] Zimmermann J, Kerber A, Rek K, Hopwood CJ, Krueger RF. A brief but comprehensive review of research on the alternative DSM-5 model for personality disorders. Current Psychiatry Reports. 2019;**21**(9):92

[10] Livesley WJ, Jang KL, Jackson DN, Vernon PA. Genetic and environmental contributions to dimensions of personality disorder. The American Journal of Psychiatry. 1993;**150**(12):1826-1831

[11] Kendler KS, Aggen SH, Czajkowski N, Røysamb E, Tambs K, Torgersen S, et al. The structure of genetic and environmental risk factors for DSM-IV personality disorders: A multivariate twin study. Archives of General Psychiatry. 2008;**65**(12):1438-1446

[12] Fonagy P, Luyten P. A developmental, mentalization-based approach to the understanding and treatment of borderline personality disorder. Development and Psychopathology. 2009;**21**(4):1355-1381

[13] Krueger RF, Markon KE. The role of the DSM-5 personality trait model in moving toward a quantitative and empirically based approach to classifying personality and psychopathology. Annual Review of Clinical Psychology. 2014;**10**:477-501

[14] Linehan MM. Cognitive-Behavioral Treatment of Borderline Personality Disorder. Vol. xvii. New York, NY, US: Guilford Press; 1993. 558 p

[15] Bateman AW, Gunderson J, Mulder R. Treatment of personality disorder. Lancet London England. 2015;**385**(9969):735-743

[16] Silbersweig D, Clarkin JF, Goldstein M, Kernberg OF, Tuescher O, Levy KN, et al. Failure of frontolimbic inhibitory function in the context of negative emotion in borderline personality disorder. The American Journal of Psychiatry. 2007;**164**(12):1832-1841

[17] Johnson BN, Vanwoerden S. Future directions in personality pathology development research from a trainee perspective: Suggestions for theory, methodology, and practice. Current Opinion in Psychology. 2021;**37**:66-71

[18] Chanen AM, McCutcheon L. Prevention and early intervention for borderline personality disorder: Current status and recent evidence. The British Journal of Psychiatry. Supplement. 2013;**54**:s24-s29

Section 2

New Strategies for Treatment in Personality Disorders

Chapter 4

Evidence-Based Psychotherapies for Borderline Personality Disorders

María-José Martín-Vázquez

Abstract

Borderline Personality Disorders have increased its prevalence in the last decades. The prognosis for these patients has improved due to the development of some psychotherapeutic techniques, which have been studied with clinical trials, demonstrating their efficacy. Though there are some other treatments with clinical trials (as EMDR), the four techniques that have more evidence and are more widely used are Dialectical Behavioral Therapy (DBT), Transference-Focused Psychotherapy (TFP), Mentalization Based Therapy (MBT), and Good Psychiatric Management (GPM). None of them has demonstrated to be superior to the others, but their indication can be different in function of the symptomatology, the characteristics of the patients, or the moment of the disorder.

Keywords: borderline personality disorder, dialectical behavioral therapy, transference based psychotherapy, mentalization based therapy, good psychiatric management, EMDR

1. Introduction

In recent years, the number of patients diagnosed with personality disorders has increased significantly, despite not being included in the classifications of mental illnesses until 1980. The overall prevalence is around 9% of the population [1].

In many cases, patients have one or more diagnoses of personality disorders and may seek help when they have other Axis I symptoms, usually anxiety or depressive symptoms. So, comorbidity is the rule, more than an exception. Personality disorders would correspond to a pathological extreme on a continuum from adaptive personality to severe personality disorder [2].

Personality could be defined as the more or less stable organization of affect, cognition, and behavior of a person that determines their adaptation to their environment. In personality, there is a biological and neurochemical substrate (temperament) that is influenced by learning, upbringing, and environment [3].

Temperament can be observed practically from birth and is stable from childhood to adulthood: calm, restless, difficult children. It is moderately inherited, up to 50% [2].

Character would be the non-automatic and intentional part of personality and develops from learning in the environment. It consists of values, goals, coping strategies, and beliefs about oneself and the environment.

$$\text{Personality} = \text{Temperament} + \text{Character}$$

Personality disorders usually appear during childhood or adolescence. In severe or prolonged stressful situations, severe psychiatric disorders, or brain injuries during adulthood, personality transformations can occur on a previously adapted or "normal" personality.

Personality can be defined based on different factors or dimensions. There are several models that describe different factors. Among these models, we can highlight Cloninger's 7-dimensional model: 4 temperamental factors, with a more biological and inheritable basis, and another 3 factors dependent on character [2].

Temperamental dimensions are responsible for automatic responses to memories and emotions that appear unconsciously. The caudate nucleus and the putamen are involved in these traits; they are inherited independently between 50 and 65% [1]:

- Novelty seeking: a tendency to respond strongly to new stimuli and reward signals that lead to exploratory activity. People who score high in this dimension get bored easily, are impulsive, and tend to improvise. Novelty seeking at the brain level is mediated by dopamine.

- Harm avoidance: people who score high in this trait avoid exposing themselves to new situations for fear of physical and emotional harm, respond intensely to aversive signals or stimuli, and learn to inhibit behaviors to avoid punishment and frustration.

- Reward dependence: a need for attachment and social affiliation, socially dependent, sentimental, and in need of approval.

- Persistence: the ability to maintain continuous effort to achieve long-term goals. It is mediated by norepinephrine.

Character dimensions involve the conscious and voluntary retrieval of memories, and the brain area involved is the hippocampus:

- Self-directedness: people who score high in this trait take responsibility for their actions without blaming others, are disciplined, and have goals. People with personality disorders have low self-directedness.

- Cooperativeness: people with empathy, social tolerance, compassion, and ethical and moral principles.

- Self-transcendence: intuition, imagination, spirituality, and idealism.

To make a diagnosis of personality disorder, abnormal behavior must be long-lasting, affect several aspects of personality [affectivity, way of relating to others, impulse control, style of perceiving and thinking), be generalized and maladaptive, and cause personal distress (although it may arise very late) and impairment in social and professional performance (which may not appear).

In a very simplistic way, we could talk about neurobiological determinants of some personality dimensions: impulsivity has been associated with decreased serotonin, increased excitatory amino acids such as NMDA and AMPA, norepinephrine, dopamine, and vasopressin, and decreased impulsivity with serotonin, opioids, and GABA. Aggressiveness has also been related to decreased serotonin, as well as harm avoidance and anxiety. Novelty seeking seems to be mediated by dopamine. These approaches are important when establishing psychopharmacological treatment in people with personality disorders [1, 2].

Childhood trauma situations, such as sexual or physical abuse, neglect, abandonment, severe illness of one of the parents, or social adversity, have also been related to the development of personality disorders, so these are circumstances that should be taken into account in primary care when detected so that early intervention can be made. They are mainly related to Group B disorders (borderline, histrionic, and antisocial) [4].

Other factors influencing the development of a personality disorder include the attachment model with caregivers, especially the mother [5].

Social and environmental factors also favor the expression of different personality disorders.

2. Treatment of borderline personality disorder (BPD)

Among all the personality disorders, the probability of seeking help in clinical settings is higher for Borderline Personality Disorder (BPD) than for the others. Though in the past, there was a lack of hope for the treatments, nowadays, several therapeutic techniques have shown evidence of efficacy. BPD implies a high degree of functional deficiencies in several fields: interpersonal relationships, identity, and affectivity. Among the behavioral manifestations, self-destructive and suicidal behavior are significant in the clinical presentation.

Since the illness incurs high costs due to the use of social and health systems, it has significant socio-health relevance. Therefore, it is not surprising that so many theoretical and empirical works have been published about BPD, except for antisocial personality disorder.

The prevalence of BPD is 1–2% in the general population, 10% in outpatients, and 15–25% in hospitalized psychiatric patients. A significant public health problem associated to BDP is suicidality, as 8–10% of patients with BPD finally die by suicide, though the rate of suicidal attempts is much higher. BDP appears more commonly in women, as men with BPD tend to be more hetero-aggressive than self-aggressive, which means they may receive other diagnoses or appear in different settings [6].

Phenomenological diagnosis and classification are generally carried out according to the International Classification of Mental Disorders (ICD-11) or the Diagnostic and Statistical Manual of Mental Disorders (DSM-5). Diagnostic criteria have been conceptualized clinically-theoretically and not empirically [7].

Comorbidity among different personality disorders is very high; that is, certain patients often have multiple personality disorders. Therefore, the categories are not well-defined, with low discriminant validity, and patients within a category are very heterogeneous, conditioned by the multiple possibilities of combining different individual diagnostic criteria. The different elements are weighted equally, although they may have different clinical and diagnostic relevance.

The diagnostic criteria for personality disorders have been revised in DSM-V [1, 3, 7], a classification with 5 levels of severity for diagnosing personality disorders:

Levels of Personality Functioning Scale. It differentiates disorders in the *functional areas of the self* with dimensions *of identity and self-direction*, as well as the *interpersonal area* with dimensions of *empathy and intimacy*. Only six specific personality disorders are finally detailed in DMS 5: *antisocial, avoidant, borderline, narcissistic, obsessive-compulsive, and schizotypal*. All others are defined as personality disorders diagnosed by specific traits. DMS 5 develops personality traits and facets to describe the rest of the personality disorders. Five personality traits are described for the differentiated determination of personality disorders: *negative affectivity, detachment, antagonism, disinhibition vs. compulsivity, and psychoticism*. Several facets define each personality trait. For example, negative affectivity includes emotional lability, anxiousness, separation insecurity, perseveration, submissiveness, hostility, depressivity, suspiciousness, and restricted affectivity.

In transference-focused psychotherapy (TFP) [8, 9], the diagnosis of structure, referred to by the functional level of personality in DSM-V, plays a key role. Both the basic etiological assumptions and those related to the developmental psychology of TFP, as well as the diagnostic and therapeutic approach, explicitly refer to deficiencies in the structure (functional level) of personality.

BPD has a very high comorbidity rate with other mental illnesses: in a year, 84.5% suffer one or more Axis I disorder, and 73.9% have a lifetime diagnosis of one or more comorbid personality disorders [9]. The high comorbidity rate with post-traumatic stress disorder (PTSD) is noteworthy: 39.2% of all patients with BPD are affected.

The four therapies that have shown evidence in the treatment of BPD are dialectical behavior therapy (DBT), mentalization-based therapy (MBT), transference-focused psychotherapy (TFP), and Good/General Psychiatric Management (GPM). EMDR treatment has also shown its usefulness in the therapy of patients with BPD, although it is not developed for this disorder, and its utility is likely focused on patients with early trauma [8].

3. Characteristics of the four evidence-based therapies

See **Table 1**.

	Dialectical behavior therapy (DBT)	**Mentalization-based therapy (MBT)**	**Transference-focused psychotherapy (TFP)**	**General psychiatric management (GPM)**
Description	Modified cognitive-behavioral therapy with validation and dialectical techniques. Training skills in emotional regulation, interpersonal relationships, distress tolerance, and mindfulness	"Not knowing" and curiosity as mean therapist position. Increase ability to think about oneself and others, understanding meaningful mental states	Surges from psychoanalysis, tries to integrate splitting object relations to improve relationships with oneself and others	Integrates psychodynamic and behavioral models with case management approach, focusing on interpersonal and situational stressors.

	Dialectical behavior therapy (DBT)	Mentalization-based therapy (MBT)	Transference-focused psychotherapy (TFP)	General psychiatric management (GPM)
Therapy time requirements per week:	3 h (1 individual +2 group)	3 h (1 individual +2 group)	2 h individual	1 individual.
Therapist supervision per week:	2 hours	1 h	1 h	1.5
Total weekly hours:	+5 h	4 h	3 h	2.5 h

Modified from Choin-Kain et al. (2016).

Table 1.
Characteristics of the four evidence-based therapies.

4. Dialectical behavior therapy (DBT)

Dialectical Behavior Therapy (DBT) was developed by Marsha Linehan based on her clinical experience with highly suicidal patients who did not respond to cognitive-behavioral therapy. So, Linehan added components of dialectics and validation to improve the efficacy of standard cognitive-behavioral therapy. Dialectics, which surged in ancient Greek and was developed in philosophy and repopularized by Hegel, refers to the opposition of truths, thesis, and antithesis, which must be resolved through synthesis. This approach facilitates the thinking in BPD with its black-and-white functioning, relationship problems, and polarities in its presentation. Linehan also emphasizes the need for validation as a motivation against the imperative of change, to improve the compromise of the patient in the therapy [5, 8, 10–15].

DBT formulates the problems of the disorder from a transactional model. Individuals born with high emotional sensitivity encounter invalidating environments, caregivers who are unable to perceive, understand, or effectively respond to their vulnerabilities. The disorder surges in the transaction between an emotionally sensitive individual and an invalidating environment. It causes people with high emotional sensitivity to feel that their environment cannot understand their needs and their feelings and even feel that they are punished because of their emotions, so they tend to blame others for their distress and their lives become unbearable. This process of emotional destabilization leads to cognitive, behavioral, and interpersonal regulation problems. Additionally, these sensitive individuals lack the skills to manage their hypersensitivity and usually respond to the environment ineffectively.

DBT is a structured therapy that considers the individual's problems and how they can be more effective in achieving their goals. DBT has several published volumes with extensive manualization and worksheets and is a treatment system easily understandable for therapists.

The efficacy of DBT is indisputable, but it is controversial whether so much treatment is needed to help patients recover from BPD, due to the length of the therapy and the need of supplementary homework.

The DBT model considers emotional dysregulation as the centre of a variety of emotional, cognitive, relational, identity, and behavioral problems.

Emotional dysregulation increases or exacerbates behavioral dysregulation (as out-of-control acts, impulsivity, self-injuries), cognitive dysregulation (thinking about problems and problem-solving), interpersonal dysregulation (relationship difficulties), and self-dysregulation (self-esteem, identity, negative self-perception problems).

Many problematic behaviors that appear simultaneously, such as self-injury, suicide attempts, depression, anxiety, eating disorders, PTSD, substance abuse, and aggression, can be considered dysfunctional attempts to control dysregulation and consequences of dysregulation.

When chain analysis is completed, the factor that triggers and follows the behavior to be changed is understood. But that does not achieve the expected change. Strategies for such change must be learned.

The DBT model offers several types of solutions. People diagnosed with borderline personality disorder have low clarity and awareness of what they are feeling, a general fear of emotions, and seem to use avoidant emotional regulation strategies [16].

Low self-esteem has been related to significant deficits in affective regulation [17]. Emotional regulation includes those "external and internal processes responsible for monitoring, evaluating, and modifying our emotional reactions to achieve our goals" [18]. Learning of skills includes:

- Helping to learn new psychological, emotional, and social skills.
- Generalizing these skills to real situations that have elicited less effective responses in the past.
- Collaborating on treatment goals and improving motivation to replace dysfunctional behaviors with more skilful ones.
- Managing social and family relationships to achieve more support, understanding, and validation.
- Improving therapists' skills.

General objective of DBT model is to improve clients' well-being in their daily lives.

And specific objectives are:

- Interpersonal chaos: interpersonal effectiveness skills.
- Affects emotions and labile moods: emotional regulation skills.
- Impulsivity: distress tolerance skills.
- Confusion about the self, cognitive dysregulation: basic awareness skills.

DBT skills are used to achieve the previous specific objectives:

- Mindfulness: improve attentional control without judgment. Positive self-concept.

DOI: http://dx.doi.org/10.5772/intechopen.1012489

- Emotional regulation: understand emotions, increase positive ones, accept negative ones, and improve negative experiences.

- Interpersonal skills: improve empathy and relationships while maintaining self-respect.

- Distress tolerance: tolerate unpleasant experiences without acting impulsively.

- Wise mind: balance conflicting interests, goals, and perspectives.

- Dialectics: Balance between:

    - Acceptance and validation with change.

    - Warm and careful communication with irreverent, insistent, and fact-based communication.

    - Emotion with reason.

    - The DBT therapist constantly seeks balance between tensions, the synthesis of opposites: acceptance vs. change, emphasis on deficits vs. emphasis on strengths. The goal is for the patient to abandon dichotomous thinking, accepting that reality is complex and full of contradictions and that change is the natural state. To convey this vision, the therapist may use paradoxical interventions such as the "devil's advocate technique," where they defend the symptom or behavior they actually intend to change. Metaphors, parables, myths, stories, and slogans are also used for this purpose. One of the most common, "learning to make lemonade when life gives you lemons," precisely reflects this balance between accepting life as it presents itself and making an effort to change things.

- Validation: is one of the fundamental pillars of treatment. The therapist will strive to convey to patients that their responses make sense in their context. Validation is conveyed by showing genuine interest in the patient and expressing interest and reflection on what they share. Seeking the causes and positive aspects of actions are also therapeutic strategies that can be used for validation.

- Finally, the therapist must consider the patient as someone similar to themselves, deserving of respect, and capable of change and must be willing to encourage them from this perspective.

- Emphasis on problem-solving: as a complement to validation and acceptance, the therapist will consider all symptoms, even severe ones like aggression and suicide attempts, as problems to be solved. In this sense, they will use behavioral analysis and solution analysis as tools to find alternative, healthy ways to solve problems.

    - Classical cognitive-behavioral techniques, such as the use of contingencies, can also help with this purpose.

- Empathetic and irreverent communication: DBT combines a realistic, irreverent, and paradoxical attitude toward dysfunctional behaviors, such as parasuicidal ones, with notable warmth, flexibility, close attention, and strategic self-disclosure by the therapist. Once again, the therapist maintains the balance between two seemingly opposing therapeutic styles.

1. Interpersonal skills:

   a. How to get what you want

      i. DEAR (What skills): Describe; Express; Assert; Reinforce

      ii. MAN (How skills): Mindful; Appear Confidence; Negotiate

   b. GIVE—How to maintain relationships: Gentle; Interested; Validated; Easy Manner

   c. FAST—How to maintain your self-respect: Fair; Apologizing; Stick to Values; Truthful

2. Emotion regulation:

   a. Understanding emotions

   b. Modifying unwanted emotions

   c. Reducing vulnerability:

      i. ABC skills: Accumulate positives; Build mastery; Cope ahead

      ii. PLEASE skills: treat Physical iLlness; Eating; Avoid altering drugs; Sleep; Exercise

   d. Managing extreme emotions

3. Core mindfulness skills:

   a. Wise mind

   b. What skills

   c. How skills

4. Distress tolerance skills:

   a. Surviving crises:

      i. STOP: Stop; Take a step back; Observe; Proceed mindfully

      ii. TIP: Temperature; Intense exercise; Paced breathing

iii. IMPROVE: Imagine; Meaning; Prayer; Relaxing actions; One thing; Vacation; Encouragement

iv. ACCEPTS skills: Activities; Contributing; Comparisons; Emotions; Push away; Thoughts; Sensations

b. Reality acceptance:

i. Radical acceptance

ii. Mindfulness

iii. Willingness vs. wilfulness

iv. Physical attitude.

5. Mentalization-based treatment (MBT)

According to the mentalization-based treatment model, BPD symptoms arise from the resurgence of pre-mentalizing psychic functioning modes, which appear in response to hyperactivation of the attachment system that leads to suppression of the mentalizing function [8, 16 19–23].

Mentalization is a mental process through which intentions are attributed to others and one's own intentions are recognized; it is the way we can understand that others and ourselves are driven by underlying motivations, recognizing that these take the form of different thoughts, beliefs, desires, emotions, and so on.

One of the requirements for maintaining good interpersonal relationships is that we understand each other and ourselves reasonably accurately.

The capacity for mentalization is closely related to the attachment system. In patients with BPD, insecure attachment is often found, especially disorganized attachment. The development of the agent self-representation requires others to perceive the baby as a person who thinks, feels, and acts and for the baby to be aware that they are perceived this way. Babies learn to differentiate their affective states through the signals they receive from attachment figures: parents respond by mirroring, reflecting the affect contingently and congruently, and this reflection must be marked. If not, the child may develop a disorganized attachment style. If it works well, the baby acquires a certain sense of control and self-efficacy and will later be able to symbolically represent this internal state. If the reflection is unmarked, typical BPD projective identification may appear, and if it is not congruent, a *simulated psychic functioning* may develop, leading to pseudo-mentalizing discourse. In the face of incongruent reflection, incongruent representations are internalized as part of their self-representation, giving rise to the *"alien self"*: feelings and thoughts are detected that are known to be one's own but are not experienced as authentic. The *teleological mode* in mentalization involves interpreting the actions of others, or one's own, literally, without considering the intentions, thoughts, or desires that might be behind those actions. It focuses on the visible and tangible, ignoring the internal dimension of the mind.

Social norms and those objects and meanings cognitively opaque to the child are transmitted through trust, "epistemic trust," which is a specifically human characteristic that has allowed our species to create cumulative social knowledge by ensuring effective transfer of sociocultural knowledge to each other, as all members are preconfigured from birth to "teach" and "learn." Communication based on epistemic trust is characterized by explicitly recognizing the listener. Thus, a child with secure attachment will treat his/her caregiver as a reliable source of knowledge and will also transfer and generalize that trust to other people who are in a position to teach and from whom to learn.

BPD symptoms appear as a result of partial and specific suppression of mentalization, which occurs in situations of high emotional activation, especially in intense attachment relationships and more so when there are early traumas. The child avoids thinking about the mental states of the other because it is unbearable. Hyperactivation of the attachment system leads to seeking proximity to an attachment figure, but if this figure is abusive, the brain structures involved in mentalization (frontal area) are inhibited. Suppression of mentalization causes pre-mentalizing modes to emerge: psychic equivalence and simulated mode.

Mentalization allows us to have a representation of ourselves as agents and enables us to interpret the behaviors of others based on their mental states and in psychological terms (interpretative interpersonal function). The two primitive pre-mentalizing modes of psychic functioning are *psychic equivalence* (internal and external reality are confused, fantasy is experienced as real) and *simulated mode* (dissociation between mental states and physical reality, between internal and external). Mentalization is achieved when internal representation and reality are integrated: reality is represented quite accurately, but at the same time, they are kept separate. Mentalizing involves balancing these aspects of mental function, so excessive use of any of them leads to low-quality mentalization. Relying too much on emotional stimuli is unreliable; on the contrary, relying on cognitive understanding (thoughts) without paying attention to subjective feelings will also cause problems: *hypermentalization*. Weak mentalization capacity makes a person more vulnerable to external changes and pressures.

Mentalization dysfunctions often produce misinterpretations of mental states.

The deterioration of emotional regulation means that one remains stuck in a painful, uncomfortable, and often confusing emotional state, possibly resorting to drastic means to try to escape it. Such emotional states can lead to highly self-destructive acts.

Fonagy writes about BPD in terms of instability in mentalization. Fonagy redefines the term mentalization to explain the complex capacity that a human being develops to understand the mental activity underlying social interactions, and oneself thinking, following philosophical, neuroscientific, and psychoanalytic concepts. When the mentalization is robust, it enables the individual to understand, name, and manage the number of thoughts, feelings, desires, and intentions that oneself and others have in social interactions. MBT focuses on the reciprocal relationship between secure attachment and mentalization capacity, based on developmental and attachment psychology. A limited or an unstable mentalization produces social and cognitive vulnerability, as seen in autism or BPD. Fonagy and Bateman propose that people with BPD have unstable mentalization related to their insecure and disorganized attachment. Attachment styles related to BPD are anxious, fearful, and disorganized. When the attachment system is activated, the conflict between need and fear appears, with negative attributions about oneself and others, and attachment behaviors alternating between hostility and helplessness. Thus, patients' symptoms appear when they stop mentalizing, in the face of high-intensity emotions and confusing interpersonal interactions. This means that patients have an altered view of themselves and others, unaffected by reality.

Attachment and stress response systems are hyperactivated by the stress of the attachment system, that is increased by impulsivity, paranoia, anger, suicidality, tendency to idealize or devalue, and efforts to avoid abandonment, perpetuating instability and inability to mentalize.

MBT is based on techniques aimed at stabilizing mentalization in stressful situations when the attachment system is activated. The MBT therapist takes a position of curiosity and "not knowing" to help the patient closely examine the situations that affect them, what they are thinking and feeling about themselves and others within an interpersonal interaction. The objective of MBT is to generate alternative perspectives that are less threatening, which can lead to less aggressive and more conciliatory actions. Instead of using dialectics as in DBT, it focuses on balancing mentalizing polarities: self-orientation versus other-orientation, certainty versus doubt, automatic beliefs versus more controlled and thoughtful reflections, cognitions versus emotions. MBT uses continuous assessment of attachment activation and mentalization capacity, which is a distinctive aspect of this approach. Therapists can hyperactivate the attachment system and conflicts, but with caution and kindness. The balance must be observed between activating the attachment system sufficiently to allow mentalization, but not so much that it becomes impossible.

Dimensions of mentalization:

- Automatic/controlled

- Emotions/thoughts. Both modes of functioning are necessary, and the context dictates which is the most appropriate.

    - *Cognition*: Discussing fast or slow ways of evaluating events and interactions with people. The slower method is cognitive and involves thinking rationally and examining evidence relatively impartially. We use this method when we want to solve a problem.

    - *Affect*: Subjectivity, or "gut reaction," is a much faster way of evaluating situations, although not necessarily worse.

- Other/self

- External/internal

    - *External*: external and behaviural information. Generally, we improve our understanding of others when we consider not only their external appearance but also their internal state. To know it, we often have to use explicit mentalization.

    - *Internal*: Refers to our current internal state, that is, how we feel and what we think about something, which we can manifest to others or conceal so they do not know how we feel or what we are thinking.

- Implicit/explicit:

    - *Implicit*: when we interact with others naturally and spontaneously, mentalization occurs automatically. We do not need to make an effort and do not even realize we are mentalizing.

o *Explicit:* We can think about ourselves or others quite openly. This is something we do by verbalizing our reflections on what we feel and think, taking the context into account.

MBT warns against making complex interventions when patients are not mentalizing, such as complicated safety plans or psychodynamic interpretations. These interventions tend to cause a simulated mode in which patients are participating in a conversation "talking the talk", but they cannot connect to their real personal experiences, and it has no sense. The therapist may feel satisfied with an intervention that does not help the patient, so they must be attentive to this and reinstall mentalization so that the patient can think about their symptoms and problems; the objective for the patient is to reach a greater capacity to have a meaningful, realistic, and self-generated perspective on their own life.

The treatment strategies proposed by Bateman and Fonagy can be summarized as follows:

- Promote mentalization: the therapist must maintain a mentalizing position, reflecting on the relationship between the external and internal that can be inferred and their own internal states, staying in the here and now.

- Bridge gaps, promoting reflective processes, so that the patient can integrate their experiences and assign them a meaning that fits their narrative. The goal is for the patient to feel that the therapist has "their mind in mind."

- Work with current mental states: trying to discover how current mental states may be influenced by past events.

- Take into account the patient's deficits. In general, the intervention will be more supportive if the emotional intensity of the moment is very high, but if affects can be contained, mentalization will be deepened.

From less to more depth, the following interventions can be used:

- Reassurance, support, and empathy clarification

- Challenge and elaboration affects basic mentalization:

  o "stop, listen, look,"

  o "stop, rewind, explore"

- Interpretative mentalization: the therapist offers an alternative perspective to what the patient says, relating the patient's reaction to a mental state.

- Transfer mentalization: encourages the patient to reflect on the relationship with the therapist in the present, so that they focus their attention on the other's mind and contrast their own perception of how they are seen by the other.

The treatment is structured in three phases: the initial phase includes the assessment of the patient's mentalization capacity, attempts to achieve patient adherence to treatment, and concludes with case formulation, which is shared in writing with the patient; the second phase or middle phase is individual and group therapy aimed at working on mentalization, and the final phase, usually after 12–18 months of therapy, involves preparation to end intensive treatment.

Compared to DBT, MBT requires less training and fewer time resources and does not require "homework" for patients or therapists, but focuses on stabilizing mentalization capacity both inside and outside sessions.

Mentalization has been used in different settings, with different patient populations, and has even been integrated into other therapeutic strategies. Since it is less manualized than other strategies, novice therapists may feel overwhelmed by the emotional and interpersonal intensity of patients with BPD.

The MBT model proposes a combination of individual and group therapy, as well as a mentalization team that supports therapists in mentalizing about how they react to patients. It is recommended for confident, flexible, experienced therapists with common sense, not for those who are inexperienced, anxious, or poorly relate to patients with BPD.

6. Transference-focused psychotherapy (TFP)

Transference-Focused Psychotherapy (TFP) is a psychoanalytically oriented therapy, with differences from classical psychoanalysis in that there is a prioritization of themes in the treatment, and it works mainly on the transfer relationship in the here and now [8, 9, 24–27].

It is based on the object relations theory: early internalized relational experiences would play a central role in the maturation of a person's personality, and dysfunctional or traumatic relational experiences can lead to a developmental disorder, which means that certain personality functions are configured as a disorder or a borderline structure of personality organization, leading to alterations in the perception of oneself and others in a realistic and integral way, disorganization of interpersonal relationships, impulsivity and self-directed and other-directed aggressiveness, immature defense mechanisms, and lack of internalization of moral values.

The therapy focuses on the transfer relationship, on the updating of early internalized relational experiences in the therapeutic relationship: in this relationship between the patient and the therapist, the problems of early internalized relationships will arise.

In TFP, it is assumed that the "foundations of personality" are in the early internalized relational experiences (the first three years of life); later relational experiences can also be decisive, but if development has been healthy up to that point, they are processed differently. Relational experiences are internalized especially when they are significant from an affective point of view, both positively and negatively. The integration of positive and negative affects in the perception of oneself and the object appears approximately from the age of three, which implies the acquisition of object constancy, allowing the positive aspects of the other to continue to be perceived, even if we are very angry with them at that moment. The term representation refers to the internal images that a person accumulates about themselves and others. In the case of healthy development, from the age of three, there is an integration of partial aspects into complete internal images of the self and objects. A healthy representation world is characterized by the ability to access internal images at any time, regardless of the situation and the presence of the other.

If there is a structural disorder, only internalized partial object relationships can be accessed, which subsequently determine experiences; in particular, partial object relationships with another valence cannot be accessed. The organization that occurs in the case of structural disorders is called identity diffusion and is accompanied by so-called primitive defense mechanisms:

- Splitting.
- Idealization and devaluation.
- Omnipotence.
- Primitive denial.
- Projective identification.

Kernberg [28, 29] distinguishes three levels of personality organization based on the three criteria of identity integration, the maturity of defense mechanisms, and the capacity for reality testing: healthy or neurotic, borderline, and psychotic. In this model, it is important to distinguish the terms borderline personality organization and borderline personality disorder. The first designates the level of structural integration, while the second is a nosological entity (**Table 2**).

The goal of the structural interview is the categorical and individual diagnosis of the structure (STIPO). The interview provides a structural profile of the personality, as well as an overall assessment of the structural level with the following six levels: normal, neurotic 1, neurotic 2, borderline 1, borderline 2, and borderline 3.

The STIPO assesses seven dimensions:

- Identity (Commitment, Self-perception, Coherence and continuity, Self-evaluation, Object perception)
- Object relations (Interpersonal relationships, Couple and sexuality, Internal working model of relationships)
- Primitive defenses
- Rigidity
- Aggression (Self-aggression, hetero-aggressiveness)
- Moral values
- Reality perception.

Identity	Reality testing	Defense mechanisms
Neurotic Structures	Integrated	Present
Borderline Structures	Identity Diffusion	Present
Psychotic Structures	Split	Absent

Table 2.
Levels of personality organization.

TFP has been developed for the treatment of all personality disorders located at the lower level of borderline organization, except for antisocial personality disorder, as the dishonesty characteristic of this disorder prevents them from fulfilling the therapeutic contract. TFP has developed also a model to treat narcissistic personality disorder, based on the BDP treatment, modified.

For clinical diagnosis, TFP continues to use the structural interview, which allows for a diagnosis of transference and a deeper psychodynamic understanding. In the diagnosis, special attention is paid to previous treatments, the reasons for therapy failures, and aspects that may pose a potential threat to the therapy. After completing the diagnosis, the patient is informed about it and the treatment options, before being explained the specific particularities of the therapeutic configuration and procedure. If, within the framework of shared decision-making with the patient, a decision is made in favor of TFP, the therapeutic contract is discussed, and therapy does not begin until the contract is definitively concluded.

The therapeutic contract serves to ensure that therapy takes place regularly and that the patient can actively participate in it. Possible threats to the patient's life or others, as well as dangers to the therapy, are contractually regulated based on the information gathered during the anamnesis.

The possibility of observing and analyzing the patient's relational experience and behavior "live" provides a valuable opportunity to improve their self-perception and relationships, as well as to integrate their identity.

It is assumed that patients with borderline disorder do not transfer complete objects but aspects of internalized partial object relationships. At the same time, the patient lives in the complementary role of the internalized partial object relationship. At a given moment, only one relationship dyad is activated in the transference, which dominates everything, and a role reversal or role change can quickly occur. The goal of TFP is to accommodate these transference processes within the therapy and identify, name, and analyze them with the patient. From the repeated updates of the different transference dyads and, especially, the role reversals, it can be seen that both parts of the dyad really come from the patient's inner world.

The following *TFP techniques* are used for analysis:

- Clarification
- Confrontation
- Interpretation
- Working through

Once this is done to the necessary extent, integration of the fragmented parts of the self or objects can take place, resulting in structural maturation.

Strategic Principles of TFP:

- Definition of dominant object relations:
    - Phase 1: Experience and tolerate the confusion of the patient's internal world.
    - Phase 2: Detect dominant object relations.

  - o Phase 3: Name the actors.
  - o Phase 4: Observe the patient's reaction.

- Observe the patient's role changes.
- Observe and interpret the relationships between mutually rejecting object relation dyads that maintain internal conflict and fragmentation.
- Work on the patient's ability to perceive a relationship in the transference differently and observe the patient's other relevant relationships in light of this change.

Tactics: The term tactical procedure summarizes the four individual treatment phases in TFP, which must be applied from one session to another to ensure the framework and progress of the therapy so that therapeutic work can take place without obstacles.

Tactical elements of TFP:

- Therapeutic contract
- Prioritization of themes and selection of the main theme from the material provided by the patient
- Highlighting incompatible realities based on a common reality
- Emotion regulation

TFP follows a list of priorities, which establishes that those disorders that prevent or hinder therapeutic work must be discussed and worked on first. In this sense, the first priority is ensuring the survival of the patient and the therapist, followed by patient behaviors that could lead to therapy suspension. Additionally, patient behaviors that prevent constructive work in therapy are analyzed. Until all these threats are overcome, work on the transference does not begin. Therefore, the therapist must keep these priorities in mind and constantly check if there is a danger to the therapy, which must be addressed immediately.

If no transference material is manifested, work will be done where the patient's most intense affect resides.

A common reality must be created when the patient's perception of reality is not compatible with the therapist's one. In the context of incompatible realities, this attempt would not be appropriate.

The TFP therapist assumes a position of technical neutrality, maintaining equidistance concerning all the patient's internal efforts, not valuing them, and trying to help the patient make a free decision in favor of one way or another. Technical neutrality must be temporarily abandoned in certain circumstances in TFP. The therapist's change of technical neutrality occurs whenever, within the framework of the priority list, the therapy or its context is threatened or hindered, or if a temporary abandonment of neutrality is required to take a stand against a strongly destructive inner part of the patient.

The TFP technique corresponds to that of other psychoanalytic therapies: clarification, confrontation, interpretation, and working through. Using interpretations and integrating the information obtained from clarification and confrontation connects the patient's conscious material with the supposed, hypothetical, unconscious material, which is attributed an influence on the patient's motivation and behavior. A single interpretation, even if correct, is generally not enough to create lasting change in the patient. Usually, the same contexts must be interpreted several times, and during this process, they are worked through. This means that the patient mentally and emotionally faces the corresponding contexts, reflecting on them together with the therapist. Since these are often negative contents and stressful experiences, this also entails a painful process that requires time. Interpreting and working through are sometimes painful processes that can be prolonged over a long period.

No therapy for patients with BPD should be carried out without periodic and competent supervision. In TFP, supervision through video recordings of sessions is the norm, usually conducted as group supervision every 1–2 weeks. For this, extracts of the therapies are viewed and then discussed in a group with the supervisor. The information obtained through video recordings allows for the evaluation of non-verbal manifestations of transference, which greatly improves the effectiveness of supervision.

Transference-focused psychotherapy is a manualized, psychoanalytically oriented psychotherapy based on the conceptualization of borderline personality organization developed by Otto Kernberg. Kernberg includes in borderline organization not only BPD but also other severe personality disorders, described in cluster B's DSM, such as histrionic, narcissistic, and antisocial. The functioning of these disorders is characterized by identity diffusion (poor sense of self); primitive defense mechanisms (such as splitting); unstable sense of reality, with variable capacities for empathy and tact; aggressiveness toward oneself and others; and confused internal relationship models.

Borderline personality disorder is the result of the combination of temperamental factors, such as the tendency to have negative affectivity and low effort control, and an adverse early relational context during infancy (neglect, separation, abuse, high family conflict, or instability). One of the strengths of TFP is its explanation of personality development, from normal, mature, or immature variations to pathological. Due to this theoretical framework, TFP targets more patients than other psychotherapies developed for BPD. The goal of TFP is for patients and therapists to discuss together the problematic interpersonal dynamics that recurrently appear in the patient's life and inside the therapy, and the intense emotions that accompany them, analyzing the transference.

Individual therapy is more intense than in other approaches: ideally, two individual sessions per week and one group session. In individual therapy, the goal is to create a safe context to analyze relational patterns, revealing the patient's internal object relations, both in relationships outside and within therapy with the therapist. The way object relations are reproduced with the therapist in the transference is fully analyzed with clarification, confrontation, and interpretation techniques. The objective is to help the patient to resolve the splits between "good and bad," leading to a more integrated thinking about themselves and others.

TFP has been shown to be effective in reducing suicidality, as well as irritability and reflective functioning and attachment analysis, demonstrating the emergence of internal changes in the patients' psychology, more than other strategies.

A major strength of TFP is that it focuses more on character and less on symptoms, making it more useful for treating patients with other personality disorders.

Therapist training is more rigorous, for more experienced therapists with a background in psychodynamic therapy.

7. General / good psychiatric management (GPM)

Gunderson et al. developed GPM, considering that many mental health professionals have negative attitudes toward treating patients with borderline personality disorder (BPD), due to perceived difficulties in treating these patients. These difficulties to treat BPD are based on the perception of suicidal tendencies and the familiarity of mental health professionals with specific approaches to treat borderline personality disorder. This means that many patients with BPD are left out of treatments that could be useful for them, which evidently leads to a worse prognosis and course of the disease [8, 22, 30–33].

In recent years, the prognosis for patients with BPD seems to have improved, and part of this improvement is attributed to the development of more generalist treatments that have shown efficacy, the most well-known being General Psychiatric Management (GPM).

GPM was developed for the intervention in outpatients who can be treated in community mental health services without much deviation from their usual work. Despite the description of GPM as Good Psychiatric Management or General Psychiatric Management, it is not developed solely for use by psychiatrists; other mental health professionals may also find this model useful.

Gunderson developed General Psychiatric Management (Good Psychiatric Management) initially with a diagnostic interview, whose criteria were used in the development of the DSM-III, and later wrote a guide on BPD, from which the therapeutic strategy GPM was developed together with Links. It is a less intensive and less specialized strategy than MBT, DBT, and TFP, but it is effective over the follow-up and with fewer dropouts.

Gunderson's formulation of BPD views the central deficit of BDP as their interpersonal hypersensitivity. When patients with BPD feel connected to an important relationship, such as the one that appears with the therapist, they will present as anxious, dependent, seeking help, and idealizing, but when they feel a real or perceived threat of being abandoned or rejected, the patients will become angry, devaluing, and self-injurious. This usually requires rescue or greater involvement from others, helping the patients return to a state of "connection." If this does not happen and others respond with more rejection, the patient will become more dissociated, suicidal, or unresponsive to the environment. A supportive environment, such as hospitalization or intensive outpatient treatment, can also help the patient return to a state of greater connection.

The goal of treatment is to help the patient to understand what emotions and thoughts are under these cycles of instability so that they can begin to think and communicate rather than react.

The natural course of BDP, overall, in their less severe presentation, is eventual remission, so GPM instructs the therapist to remain connected, interested, and focused on the interpersonal effects the therapist has on the patient and vice versa.

Accessibility between sessions is neither recommended nor contraindicated. When the patient shows improvement with mere contact, the therapist notes it and, in the next session, raises the question of whether it is a good way to manage distress. If the patient shows excessive dependence on intersession contacts, this has to be examined, and the patient is helped to develop greater attention and control over their excessive interpersonal hypersensitivity.

An important part of GPM is psychoeducation, where the clinician informs the patient about their illness, examines how symptoms evolve, and encourages adaptation and planning. A unique component of GPM, in front of the other psychotherapy approaches, is the informed management of medication and comorbid disorders. There is also an emphasis on the need to have a job, as in TFP, as it is advised that they first have a job because once they have developed a source of self-direction and identity, they are more capable of being more stable in the context of relationships ("first job, then love").

The practical guide for the treatment of patients with BPD developed by the APA (American Psychiatric Association) states that psychotherapy is the main treatment for patients with BPD, complemented with medications aimed at symptoms. GPM includes a psychotherapy component based on psychodynamic, psychotherapeutic support. The psychotherapy component emphasizes the relational aspects of the disorder and attributes the difficulties to a deficit model focused on the consequences of precarious early attachment relationships.

Interpersonal hypersensitivity, as the dynamic center of BPD, explains why patients go from feeling connected in an idealized and dependent relationship to feeling threatened when separation is perceived or actualized or feeling alone and abandoned when they experience interpersonal abandonment. The objective of the therapy is exploring the consequences of interpersonal hypersensitivity in patients' relationships and their emotional processing. As in TFP and MBT, the experience of the therapeutic relationship is seen as having a central function helping to regulate emotional regulation. The emotions that surge in therapy sessions and their validation and regulation in a relational context by the therapist help individuals to develop the capacity to self-regulate their effect and self-esteem.

GPM also includes medication management aimed at symptoms, as presented in the APA guide. One of the goals of medication is to prevent suicidality and self-injurious behaviors resulting from emotional lability and impulsivity.

The typical contract in GPM includes weekly individual sessions, during which pharmacological management is also reviewed. Sessions frequently last 50 minutes, and the therapist is accessible for crises between sessions during working hours. Outside of working hours, the patient is advised to use the crisis services available in the community.

A 2009 study by McMain [15] shows that the efficacy of GPM is similar to DBT. It is a multicenter, single-blind study involving 180 patients. Both groups showed similar levels of improvement in a variety of clinical measures, including decreases in the frequency and severity of suicidal and non-suicidal self-injuries, decreased use of healthcare services including emergency visits and hospitalizations, and improvement in BPD symptoms such as anxiety, depression, irritability, and interpersonal functioning, but GPM is less exigent in terms of time and homework.

Good Psychiatric Management (GPM) is based *on six principles*:

1. The first is that the therapist is active and avoids being reactive during therapy sessions and is curious to understand the patient and understands their responsibility to keep the patient engaged in treatment. The therapist's reliability, listening skills, sincere concern, and validation are central and non-specific therapeutic factors. Sometimes the clinician may advise that changes in patients' life situations can lead to radical clinical changes. You are the container (careful, thoughtful, resistant to projections).

2. The second principle is support and validation as crucial ingredients, especially in the initial phases of therapy. Support is provided through active listening, interest, and selective validation; the patient's description of what is happening

to them is understood as legitimate and understandable, which does not imply agreement. Sometimes it is necessary to be in a position of "not knowing." The patient is guided with the therapist's collaboration to make sense of what happened.

3. The third principle is focus on real life: on relationships and vocation. Case management is an essential aspect of this therapy, so the clinician focuses on the life outside of therapy and not primarily on the presentation in psychotherapy. In this context, the principle "work before love" is proposed: love for someone who cannot take care of themselves is rarely sustainable, and work makes one kinder.

4. Fourth, the therapeutic relationship must be dyadic, real, professional, and attentive to maintaining the therapeutic framework; sometimes, the clinician's self-disclosure of emotions and personal experiences, or even posed hypothetically, such as "if that happened to me, I would feel..." or "I would do..." would be appropriate in sessions.

5. Fifth, change is expected as part of the therapeutic contract; no specific duration or intensity of therapy is prescribed, but it is assumed that the patient should make progress toward treatment goals over time. Therefore, if this does not happen, the clinician would review with the patient the effectiveness of the current approach and plan other intervention if it is finally considered.

6. Sixth, the patient is seen as a competent adult, so the clinician expects him/her to be an active participant in all aspects and phases of treatment, which has the objective to improve and support the patient's self-agency in their life.

The approach in GPM:

- Psychoeducation is essential
- Central non-specific factors: reliability, listening, concern
- Central relational tasks: attachment, trust
- Essential situational changes: advice, assistance
- Pragmatism: each patient is different.

Psychoeducation about BPD should be provided, including discussion of genetic origins and other causes, diagnostic criteria, course, prognosis, and various treatments that may be considered. Patients' families should be included in the education, except when clinical circumstances contraindicate it. Generally, when patients receive psychoeducation about their diagnosis, they can understand that their disorder truly exists and that they will be treated seriously, and they feel reassured knowing they are not alone. This psychoeducation also speaks to the patient's healthy observer, allowing them to have a more objective view of their personal experiences and reducing internal judgments. The information about the course of the disorder helps the patient to understand that treating BPD is fundamental to prognosis because comorbid disorders, such as major depressive disorder, are unlikely to remit until BPD symptoms are treated.

A strategy used in GPM is autobiography, with the dialectical management of information, chain analysis, and observation of behavior patterns.

The therapy goals are to have a life worth living, work before love, goal setting, and short-term goals, but with great flexibility. It is interesting to anticipate the challenges that will arise, such as recurring difficulties, making a safety plan, hypersensitivity to loneliness, rejection, and decreased support.

Factors affecting risk variation are considered:

- Increase risk:
    - Negative interpersonal events
    - Substance abuse
    - Increased depression
- Decrease risk:
    - Positive interpersonal events
    - Safety plan
    - Crisis management skills
    - Hospitalization
    - Low doses of antipsychotics.

It is a multimodal approach with a general recommendation that treatment should involve at least two therapists, two modalities, or any other two components. It supports concomitant treatments, but it is important to assure a direct collaborative communication between treatment providers. Psychopharmacological management is considered an adjunct therapy for specific symptoms that are an appropriate target for it, as depressive or anxiety symptoms. Hospitalization can be used for safety and asylum (misuse can be secondary gain and avoidance) and to evaluate treatment, consider medication changes, medication withdrawal, increase family involvement, manage situational stressors, difficult disclosures, and develop discharge care plans. Clinicians should pay careful attention to their effectiveness and can and should seek negative transference and counter-transference.

Although GPM is an informed psychodynamic treatment, direct transference in the here and now interpretations are not recommended. The model assumes that patients are in deficit, in emotion processing and due to their unstable attachment, rather than a conflict-oriented perspective. Expressions of anger or rage in the here and now are understood as emotional responses, though maladaptive, and as a reflection of previous empathic failures or traumas that contribute to these deficits. In this context, early interpretations can generate a sense of shame, especially if they are not done carefully and within a stable working relationship. But negative transferences are also discussed in therapy, because hostility and negative transferences are expected and actively addressed early. As complementary negative counter-transferences surge as part of therapy, it is recommended that they be managed through discussions with trusted colleagues or supervision. This is considered an important part of GPM and is the best method to avoid transgressions, harm to the patient, and litigation.

In GPM, it is essential to address interpersonal hypersensitivity. The clinician consistently focuses on the patient's relationships and connects the patient's emotions and behaviors with interpersonal stressors. These interactions also include those that occur with the therapist in the here and now. The clinician can offer self-clarification during these emotional interactions and even apologize if distress arises due to their intervention. Very importantly, the clinician must know that erroneous interventions are inevitable, useful, and reversible.

An important task with chronically suicidal patients is to assess the intensity and potential lethality of suicidal ideation and behavior and overall acute ideation, as concerns about imminent death by suicide can cause significant anxiety for the clinician and hinder therapy. The presence of acute or chronic suicide risk should be evaluated, focusing on identifying periods when environmental factors increase the risk of suicidal behavior above the patient's baseline. In this context, the intervention on the safety plan, a protocol developed by Stanley and Brown in 2012 [34], is used. It is a brief, collaborative intervention designed to assess immediate suicide risk and create a coping plan agreed upon by both the therapist and patient. This plan should be regularly evaluated and revised to improve it and ensure it remains relevant. The plan cannot replace risk assessment and depends on a good alliance, although it can sometimes affect it if the patient feels the therapist does not trust them.

Safety management can be based on *eight basic principles*:

- Express concern, do not ignore or negotiate
- Assess the risk: differentiate non-lethal intentions from truly suicidal ones
- Develop the safety plan
- Ask what the patient thinks might help
- If necessary, hospitalization
- Clarify the precipitants (chain analysis)
- Be clear about your limits
- Discuss the case with your supervisor, do not worry alone.

And after the crisis:

- Follow-up and discussion of all safety issues
- Discussion about interpersonal stressors
- Active interpretation of non-specific reasons that provided relief
- Emphasize the unreliability of depending on your accessibility
- Problem-solving about possible alternatives.

Regarding family interventions, a hierarchy of psychoeducation, counseling, support groups, joint sessions with patients and families, and finally family therapy is proposed. The initial one should be offered to all family members. The patient is expected to make significant changes during therapy. At six weeks of therapy, the patient is expected to show less stress and dysphoria, and the clinician should also ask if they are actively participating in therapy. Before six months have passed, the patient is expected to adopt better problem-solving strategies and better introspection and to show a significant reduction in the frequency and severity of self-destructive and suicidal behaviors. At the end of 12 months of therapy, the improvement is shown in interpersonal functioning, being more capable of understanding the intentions and emotions of others and more assertive in relationships. At the end of 18 months, the patient should have objective evidence of improved social functionality related to work, schooling, or other meaningful activities. Ideally, in two years or more, the patient would no longer meet the criteria for BPD, show generalized learning, and have internalized a good "self."

At all stages, the therapeutic relationship should be assessed: Are both of you comfortable in therapy? Does your understanding and empathy as a therapist increase? Does their trust in you improve? If these changes are not observed, the patient and therapist should consider whether they should be referred to more specific therapies such as DBT, mentalization-based therapy, or transference-focused psychotherapy.

Weekly individual therapy is recommended as long as the patient benefits from it, meaning psychological, behavioral, and functional changes are observed. Psychoeducation about the disorder is also provided.

Training in GPM is the shortest and most economical of the specific BPD therapy trainings. It is also less ambitious in its objectives and format. One of the fundamental messages of GPM is inherently Hippocratic: do the least harm possible since BPD is a disorder that will likely improve or eventually remit. The message is combined with the imperative to improve functionality and quality of life.

8. Treatment options

Currently, the idea that one treatment is superior to another in all cases has been surpassed. The question is in which clinical situation one or the other could be implemented (**Tables 3** and **4**).

Among all these strategies, GPM and MBT are the ones that can be most easily combined with others. Studies have been conducted combining MBT and DBT. Mentalization is a mean component in all psychotherapeutic strategies, and DBT and MBT share many elements, strategies, or techniques, such as mindfulness, validation, the therapist's non-defensive humility, self-disclosure, and chain analysis.

TFP is probably the most difficult to combine with other models.

They can be integrated in several ways:

Step-by-step progression: using specific techniques for different symptoms or phases of treatment sequentially. It's not about rotating through all the techniques but observing the clinical situation. DBT can be the first if destructive behaviors predominate and reflective functions are unstable or under stress. When behavioral problems have stabilized, TFP can be implemented to make a deeper psychological work related to attachment and interpersonal patterns. Another approach could be to use GPM initially to achieve a greater organization, acceptation, and awareness of the patients' problems. Once this occurs, they can benefit from more intensive or

	DBT	MBT	TFP	GPM
Objectives	Abandoning the hell Effectiveness A life that is worth living	Stabilizing mentalization and bond system	Integrating the splitting object relationships. Arrive to a depressive position (tolerate the loss of ideal object)	Self- confidence First work, then love
Priorities	Suicidal behaviors that interfere with the therapy and with the quality of life	Focus on interpersonal relationships	Transference Splitted object relations	Focus on interpersonal interactions
Management of suicidability	Chain analysis All day letters	Chain analysis	Interpretation of motivation and distortions	Risk valoration Chain analysis
Crisis plan	Independence skills, then coaching skills. Minimizing emergency use.	In working hours: call the mentalization team. Out of it: emergency room.	Emergency room	Contact algorism or crisis plan

Table 3.
Treatment options.

specialized psychotherapy, such as DBT, MBT, or TFP. Finally, after the most severe symptoms have subsided, GPM offers a low-intensity and frequency care modality, with monthly or even less frequent visits.

Technical eclecticism: formulation of the patient's problems, paired with structured objectives, proposing which strategies and when they will be used. This approach is proposed by Livesly and Clarkin [22], observing common factors. The main limitation of structured and manualized treatments is that they are not flexible enough to accommodate the heterogeneity of presentations of patients with BPD. Clinical eclecticism implies that the patient can benefit from the best strategies of each type of therapy, reducing the need to fit into a specific model. The challenge is the combination of techniques, which requires a clear formulation of each patient and understanding of which of those techniques that predict the therapeutic objectives. The mandatory tasks to make the therapeutic plan include assessment, case formulation, treatment

Treatment components	TDC	MBT	TFP	GPM
Case management	++	++	+	+++
Psychoeducation	+	++	+	+++
Group therapy	Essential	Essential	No	Recommended
Individual therapy per week	1 h	1 h	2 h	1 h
Family therapy	Family connections	MBT familiar Multifamiliar groups	No. Eventually contacts.	Family psychoducation

Table 4.
Treatment components.

structuring, monitoring the therapeutic relationship, and defining specific goals in each phase. It requires an advanced knowledge and experience of the clinician team.

Synthesis: the clinician considers the shared factors of the four strategies for their work, developing a stable and productive working alliance with patients with BPD. The four therapies for BPD share the therapist's attitude and focus: they must be active and collaborative in discussing problems, avoid long silences, and avoid relying excessively on patients to organize the discussion of problems. They also share a non-defensive humility attitude that allows patients to speak openly using their own interpersonal operations. In DBT, self-disclosure involves talking about how therapists use skills in problem-solving in their lives; in MBT, self-disclosure involves talking about their own point of view to increase the patient's perspective on the interpersonal situation, illustrating that there are different ways of interpreting interpersonal relationships.

In TFP, transference is a central element, so the therapist includes themselves in the patient's fluctuating split object relation dynamics and communicates their own experience of the relationship. The TFP therapist seeks the negative forms of transference that are key to integrating the patient's intense emotions and social cognition. In GPM, clinicians openly discuss the effect patients have on themselves and vice versa to help the patient to learn about their changing way of depending on and reacting to important relationships.

Regarding the balance between support and stimulation, DBT and MBT incorporate warmth, empathy, and validation before stimulating the patient with change-oriented strategies.

TFP employs questioning strategies, such as clarification, that lead to confrontation and interpretation to push the patient to think more openly about contradictions in their relationships with others, to reduce splitting object relations.

GPM therapists are trained to be accessible and supportive while showing skepticism about levels of dependence in relationships.

All these therapeutic positions and strategies deal with balance, dialectical thinking, and integration.

Synthesis also requires experienced clinicians, and it is unclear how both synthesis and eclecticism could be taught to novice clinicians or applied in less specialized clinical settings.

Berkson's bias has been described as the tendency of therapists to see the most chronic patients or those with the worst treatment response, while milder or

Clinical state	Severity	Definition	Potential interventions
Preclinical	Subthreshold	High risk of BPD	Mild or non-specific self-regulation problems
Initial-Middle	First episode BPD	+self-injury	-suicidality
Moderate	Evident symptoms	Lack of response to basic treatment	+self-injury
Severe	Remissions and relapses	+severe self-injury	+potentially lethal suicide attempts
Chronic Persistent	No remissions	Lack of response to intervention	Lack of response to previous stage interventions

Table 5.
Step-by-step approach.

faster-responding patients would abandon therapeutic processes. This bias assumes that all patients with a diagnosis like BPD are severe, implying that they need long and intensive treatment. However, evidence suggests that the most improvement in BPD occurs in the first six months. The duration of treatments is a factor that limits treatment accessibility. From this point of view, a step-by-step approach is proposed, as explained in the following **Table 5**:

9. EMDR and BDP

Borderline Personality Disorder (BPD) is characterized by dysregulation in several areas, primarily affective instability, impulsivity, altered perception and reasoning, and difficulty maintaining interpersonal relationships, as well as symptoms such as self-harm and suicidal behavior [6, 11, 35–37].

In a significant percentage of patients with BPD, over 75%, there are traumatic situations, attachment difficulties, neglect, and other circumstances in their history that facilitate, in predisposed patients, the development of dysfunctional personality traits, such as fear of abandonment, difficulty tolerating frustration, tendency to impulsive behaviors, and the wide spectrum of symptoms that appear in people suffering from BPD.

Between 30% and 70% of people with BPD meet the criteria for the diagnosis of post-traumatic stress disorder (PTSD) [38]. For this diagnosis, exposure to a severe and grave type T event is required (an event that fulfills criteria of those described for DSM-5 PTSD diagnosis), but memories of other types of childhood traumas seem to have an important effect on the development of BPD, as “t” traumas, which are repetitive, interpersonal but not life-threatening traumas.

Processing childhood traumatic memories can be a promising approach for treating BDP patients, as it has been shown to be effective in treating memories related to emotional abuse, neglect, divorce, or physical illness, among others. In the study by Hafkemeijer et al. in 2023, relevant memories that are supposed to have influenced the development of BPD symptoms are reprocessed with an intensive approach, improving both PTSD-compatible symptoms and BPD symptoms, which were maintained throughout the follow-up.

In BPD, a series of neurobiological alterations are observed: excessive amygdala response with decreased prefrontal activity in response to negative or neutral information (especially when coexisting with PTSD), changes in the brain’s social reward system with emotional hypervigilance, changes in cortisol and oxytocin production, among others. Exposure to adverse childhood experiences has been linked to neurological alterations both in the structure and in the function of diverse brain structures, such as the hippocampus, amygdala, and prefrontal cortex, which are crucial for emotional regulation, memory formation, social behavior and decision-making. Opioid dysregulation is associated with increased sensitivity to rejection and abandonment; oxytocin dysregulation with social hypersensitivity, distrust, and antagonism; and vasopressin with irritability [39, 40].

From the Adaptive Information Processing (AIP) model, the basis of EMDR therapy, psychological problems are due to the cumulative effect of unresolved adverse and traumatic experiences [40]. Adaptive information is not always available in personality disorders, but it may be due to a lack of learning or in the form of idealization as a form of dysfunctional positive affect, which also needs to be processed.

In hospitalized patients with personality disorders with significant emotional dysregulation, coping skills acquisition and medication use are usually addressed to reduce emotional instability and associated behaviors, but not so much the trauma. However, paying attention to trauma can reduce hospitalization time and containment needs [41]. Performing EMDR in this context of high dysregulation involves longer and more frequent sessions, adjusting the model to the situation. Additionally, working with trauma has the function of reducing retraumatization that hospitalization may entail. In a hospital context, the efficacy of intensive treatment (16 sessions in 8 days) focused on trauma combining prolonged exposure and EMDR in patients with combined BPD and PTSD has also been observed, with improvement maintained up to one year after follow-up [42].

Between 33% and 79% of patients with BPD also have symptoms that meet the criteria for PTSD, and when they have both diagnoses, they tend to present more severe symptoms, lower quality of life, and more suicidal tendencies [37]. For BPD, therapies such as dialectical behavior therapy (DBT), mentalization-based therapy (MBT), transference-focused psychotherapy (TFP), and schema-focused therapy (SFT) have been recommended, but none of these focus on specific trauma treatment. EMDR treatment proves to be effective for trauma while also reducing general BPD psychopathology and improving functionality in patients with associated BPD and PTSD. EMDR improves a wide range of symptoms and personal functionality in people with personality disorders who have suffered childhood trauma. EMDR targeting adverse childhood memories, even without a PTSD diagnosis, reduces psychopathology and improves personal functioning in people with personality disorders.

One of the difficulties that can be encountered when processing memories in BPD is that there are often many target memories, and even in complex trauma, fragmentary memories and amnesia can interfere with the identification of targets [40].

Despite everything, the response is worse in patients with BPD than in people with a single PTSD diagnosis, as the former usually have more severe symptoms and greater functional impairment. It is suggested that it be implemented in the early stages of the disease and combined with specific therapies for BPD. Faced with the question of what to treat first, PTSD or BPD, it is recommended to rethink the question of which symptoms should be treated first. Although it has been suggested that EMDR therapy may be less effective in treating memories with little emotional charge, even in patients who do not meet PTSD criteria, resolving childhood trauma memories with EMDR improves symptoms and reduces the emotionality and vividness of memories, regardless of the severity of associated events [43].

Dolores Mosquera proposes criteria that can help define which targets to treat: intrusive memories and recurrent thoughts and sensations, targets related to risk behaviors for themselves or others, and current triggers that worsen symptoms or past events not associated with painful experiences [40].

EMDR can be combined with evidence-based psychotherapies for BPD, such as SFT or individual or group DBT, with programs that combine both (EMDR + DBT) [37]. In crisis situations, brief intensive trauma-focused treatment can be effective in people with BPD and PTSD diagnoses [41]. One of the poor prognosis factors in the treatment of personality disorders is the severity of childhood abuse, as these patients tend to abandon treatment early [35]. Therefore, it is a priority to address childhood trauma in early stages, and EMDR psychotherapy has proven to be effective in this.

In 2022, a randomized study protocol was published comparing trauma-focused EMDR in patients with personality disorders versus placebo (waiting list) in reducing personality disorder symptoms (TEMPO study) [35]. This study was published in

2024, with the justification that some therapists are reluctant to use trauma-focused therapy in BPD for fear of worsening; they perform reprocessing in people on the waiting list without complete preparation, observing improvement compared to people on the waiting list [43].

Even the small percentage of patients who experienced clinical exacerbation showed clinical improvement toward the end of treatment, although in most cases, this improvement appeared after the first sessions. A study protocol comparing the efficacy of treating patients with PTSD and BPD symptoms with isolated EMDR versus EMDR + DBT has also been published, not only with clinical measures but also with neurobiological measures (changes in BDNF and FKBP5, related to cortisol metabolism and neuronal neurotrophism) [44].

De Jongh [39] proposes a six-step treatment model for personality disorders:

1. Identify intrusive memories that meet criterion A for PTSD

2. Identify non-intrusive memories that meet criterion A for PTSD and intrusive memories that do not meet these criteria

3. Identify the patient's most prominent symptoms

4. Identify memories that exacerbate or cause these symptoms; for this, it is important to conduct a specific search in early childhood. Organize all memories based on the age at which they occurred, organizing them in a timeline

5. Determine the sequence for desensitization:

   a. Start with the memories identified in steps 1 and 2, creating a list according to the SUD level of the complete memory, starting with those that score the highest. The list is complemented with those from step 4

   b. Memories with equal SUDs are organized by the age of appearance, prioritizing the earliest ones

6. Treat the memories with the standard EMDR protocol, starting with the first memory on the list.

In conclusion, clinical research indicates that EMDR treatment can be an effective practice in the therapy of patients with personality disorders, especially those with a history of trauma, which is very common in this pathology. It has been found that the benefits outweigh the possible risks of retraumatization, resulting in effective and safe therapy for patients with BPD [45, 46].

Author details

María-José Martín-Vázquez[1,2,3]

1 Department of Psychiatry and Mental Health, Hospital Universitario Infanta Sofía, Spain

2 Faculty of Medicine, Health and Sports, Department of Medicine, Universidad Europea de Madrid, Spain

3 FIIB HUIS-HUHEN, Spain

*Address all correspondence to: mjmv66@gmail.com

References

[1] Boland RJ, Verduin ML, Ruiz P, editores. Kaplan & Sadock's Synopsis of Psychiatry. 12th ed. Philadelphia: Wolters Kluwer; 2022. 1 p

[2] Roca M. Trastornos de la personalidad. Ars Médica; 2004

[3] Millon T. Trastornos de la personalidad. Más allá del DSM-IV: Masson; 1999

[4] Cervera G. Trastorno límite de la personalidad. Editorial Médica Panamericana: Paradigma de la comorbilidad psiquiátrica; 2005

[5] Linehan MMM. Cognitive-Behavioral Treatment of Borderline Personality Disorder ·. Guilford Press; 1995

[6] Choi-Kain LW, Albert EB, Gunderson JG. Evidence-based treatments for borderline personality disorder: Implementation, integration, and stepped care. Harvard Review of Psychiatry. 2016;**24**(5):342-356

[7] Paris J. Treatment of Borderline Personality Disorder: Guide to Evidence Based Practice. New York: Guilford Press; 2008

[8] Stoffers JM, Völlm BA, Rücker G, Timmer A, Huband N, Lieb K. Psychological therapies for people with borderline personality disorder. Cochrane Database of Systematic Reviews. 2012;**8**:CD005652

[9] Leichsenring F, Leibing E, Kruse J, New AS, Leweke F. Borderline personality disorder. The Lancet. 2011;**377**(9759):74-84. Disponible en: https://linkinghub.elsevier.com/retrieve/pii/S0140673610614225

[10] APA. Manual Diagnóstico y Estadístico de los Trastornos Mentales. DSM-5. American Psychiatric Association; 2013

[11] Azcárate JC, Bayón C, Cabrera C, Costi C, Díaz M, García E. Guia del Trastorno Límite de la Personalidad(Guia para el profesional). Madrid: OMC- SA; 2009

[12] Azcárate JC, Bayón C, Casas R, Costi C, Melendo JJ, Montes JM. Recorriendo los límites. Guía práctica para familiares y pacientes con trastorno límite de personalidad. Madrid: Consejería de sanidad y consumo; 2005

[13] Linehan M. Manual de Entrenamiento en Habilidades DBT para el/la Consultante. Psara Ediciones. 2022

[14] Linehan MMM. Manual de Entrenamiento en Habilidades DBT para el/la Terapeuta. Psara Ediciones. 2021

[15] Mckay M, Wood JC, Bantley J. Manual práctico de Terapia Dialectico Conductual. Bilbao. 1a ed. Desclée De Brouwer; 2017

[16] McMain SF, Links PS, Gnam WH, Guimond T, Cardish RJ, Korman L, et al. A randomized trial of dialectical behavior therapy versus general psychiatric management for borderline personality disorder. The American Journal of Psychiatry. 2009;**166**(12):1365-1374. DOI: 10.1176/appi.ajp.2009.09010039

[17] Hervás G, Vázquez C. La regulación afectiva: Modelos, investigacióne implicaciones parala salud mentaly física. Revista de Psicología Generaly Aplicada. 2006;**59**(1-2):9-36

[18] Thompson RA. Emotion regulation: A theme in search of definition. Monographs of the Society for Research in Child Development [Internet]. 1994;**59**(2/3):25. Available from: https://www.jstor.org/stable/1166137?origin=crossref [citado: 3 de septiembre de 2025]

[19] Gratz KL, Myntti W, Kiel EJ, Kurtz AJ, Tull MT. Clarifying the relation between mother and adolescent borderline personality disorder symptoms: The roles of maternal and adolescent emotion regulation and maladaptive maternal emotion socialization. Personality Disorder. 2023

[20] Bateman A, Fonagy P, Campbell C, Luyten P, Debbané M. Cambridge guide to mentalization-based treatment (MBT). Cambridge Medicine. 2023

[21] Beck E, Bo S, Jørgensen MS, Gondan M, Poulsen S, Storebø OJ, et al. Mentalization-based treatment in groups for adolescents with borderline personality disorder: A randomized controlled trial. Journal of Child Psychology and Psychiatry. 2020;**61**(5):594-604

[22] Edel MA, Raaff V, Dimaggio G, Buchheim A, Brüne M. Exploring the effectiveness of combined mentalization-based group therapy and dialectical behaviour therapy for inpatients with borderline personality disorder - a pilot study. The British Journal of Clinical Psychology. 2017;**56**(1):1-15

[23] Karterud S, Pedersen G, Engen M, Johansen MS, Johansson PN, Schlüter C, et al. The MBT adherence and competence scale (MBT-ACS): Development, structure and reliability. Psychology and Psychotherapy Research Study Journal. 2013;**23**(6):705-717

[24] Livesley WJ, Dimaggio G, Clarkin JF, editores. Integrated Treatment for Personality Disorder: A Modular Approach. New York London: Guilford Press; 2016. 478 p

[25] Wilson J, Gee B, Martin N, Maxwell S, Murdoch J, Clarke T, et al. Brief Education Supported Psychological Treatment for Adolescent Borderline Personality Disorder: The BEST Feasibility RCT. Southampton (UK); 2022

[26] Doering S. Die Übertragungsfokussierte Psychotherapie (TFP) der Borderline-Persönlichkeitsstörung. Psychiatry Psychotherapy Up2date. 2012;**6**(02):97-115. DOI: 10.1055/s-0031-1277007

[27] Kernberg OF. Severe Personality Disorders: Psychotherapeutic Strategies. 8th ed. New Haven: Yale University Press; 1986. 381 p

[28] Kernberg OF. Severe Personality Disorders: Psychotherapeutic Strategies. New Haven: Yale Univ. Press; 1984. p. 381

[29] Kernberg OF. An ego psychology-object relations theory approach to the transference. Psychoanal Q [Internet]. 1987;**56**(1):197-221. Available from: https://www.tandfonline.com/doi/full/10.1080/21674086.1987.11927

[30] Mehlum L, Bateman A, Dalewijk HJ, Doering S, Kaera A, Moran PA, et al. Building a strong European alliance for personality disorder research and intervention. Borderline Personality Disorder Emotion Dysregulation. 2018;**5**:7

[31] Yeomans FE. Psicoterapia centrada en la transferencia. Bilbao: Editorial Desclée de Brouwer; 2016. p. 1

[32] Gunderson J, Masland S, Choi-Kain L. Good psychiatric management: A review. Current Opinion in Psychology.

2018;**21**:127-131. Disponible en: https://linkinghub.elsevier.com/retrieve/pii/S2352250X17301872

[33] Gunderson JG, Links PS. Handbook of Good Psychiatric Management for Borderline Personality Disorder. Washington DC: American psychiatric publ; 2014

[34] Links PS, Ross J, Gunderson JG. Promoting good psychiatric Management for Patients with Borderline Personality Disorder. Journal of Clinical Psychology. 2015;**71**(8):753-763. DOI: 10.1002/jclp.22203

[35] Setkowski K, Palantza C, van Ballegooijen W, Gilissen R, Oud M, Cristea IA, et al. Which psychotherapy is most effective and acceptable in the treatment of adults with a (sub) clinical borderline personality disorder? A systematic review and network meta-analysis. Psychological Medicine. 2023;**53**(8):3261-3280

[36] Stanley B, Brown GK. Safety planning intervention: A brief intervention to mitigate suicide risk. Cognitive and Behavioral Practice. 2012;**19**(2):256-264. Disponible en: https://linkinghub.elsevier.com/retrieve/pii/S1077722911000630

[37] Hofman S, Hafkemeijer L, De Jongh A, Starrenburg A, Slotema K. Trauma-focused EMDR for personality disorders among outpatients (TEMPO): Study protocol for a multi-Centre, single-blind, randomized controlled trial. Trials. 2022;**23**(1):196. DOI: 10.1186/s13063-022-06082-6

[38] Mosquera D. Diamantes en bruto I: Un acercamiento al Trastorno límite de personalidad. Manual informativo para profesionales, pacientes y familiares. Madrid: Pléyades; 2004

[39] Wilhelmus B, Marissen MAE, Van Den Berg D, Driessen A, Deen ML, Slotema K. Adding EMDR for PTSD at the onset of treatment of borderline personality disorder: A pilot study. Journal of Behavior Therapy and Experimental Psychiatry. 2023;**79**:101834. Disponible en: https://linkinghub.elsevier.com/retrieve/pii/S0005791623000010

[40] Hafkemeijer L, Slotema K, Haard ND, Jongh AD. Case report: Brief, intensive EMDR therapy for borderline personality disorder: Results of two case studies with one year follow-up. Frontiers in Psychiatry. 2023;**14**:1283145. DOI: 10.3389/fpsyt.2023.1283145/full

[41] De Jongh A, Hafkemeijer L, Hofman S, Slotema K, Hornsveld H. The AIP model as a theoretical framework for the treatment of personality disorders with EMDR therapy. Frontiers in Psychiatry. 2024;**15**:1331876. DOI: 10.3389/fpsyt.2024.1331876/full

[42] Mosquera D. Treating personality disorders with EMDR therapy. Clinical Neuropsychiatry. 2018;**15**(3):187-193

[43] Winkler O, Burback L, Greenshaw AJ, Jin J. Shifting to trauma-informed Care in Inpatient Psychiatry: A case study of an individual with dissociative PTSD undergoing EMDR therapy. Case Reports in Psychiatry. 2023:1-6. Disponible en: https://www.hindawi.com/journals/crips/2023/8161010/

[44] Kolthof KA, Voorendonk EM, Van Minnen A, De Jongh A. Effects of intensive trauma-focused treatment of individuals with both post-traumatic stress disorder and borderline personality disorder. European Journal of Psychotraumatology. 2022;**13**(2):2143076. DOI: 10.1080/20008066.2022.2143076

[45] Hafkemeijer L, De Jongh A, Starrenburg A, Hoekstra T, Slotema K. EMDR treatment in patients with personality disorders. Should we fear symptom exacerbation? European Journal of Psychotraumatology. 2024;**15**(1):2407222. DOI: 10.1080/20008066.2024.2407222

[46] Snoek A, Beekman ATF, Dekker J, Aarts I, Van Grootheest G, Blankers M, et al. A randomized controlled trial comparing the clinical efficacy and cost-effectiveness of eye movement desensitization and reprocessing (EMDR) and integrated EMDR-dialectical behavioural therapy (DBT) in the treatment of patients with post-traumatic stress disorder and comorbid (sub)clinical borderline personality disorder: Study design. BMC Psychiatry. 2020;**20**(1):396. DOI: 10.1186/s12888-020-02713-x

Chapter 5

Schema Therapy for Chronic Depression: Addressing Childhood Trauma and Personality Pathology

Ayse Dondu

Abstract

Schema Therapy is an integrative psychotherapy approach originally developed for treatment-resistant patients and those with chronic psychological conditions rooted in early experiences. This chapter explores the conceptual underpinnings of Schema Therapy, including the development and maintenance of early maladaptive schemas (EMSs), schema modes, and schema coping styles. Emphasis is placed on the relationship between EMSs and depressive disorders, particularly chronic depression. The chapter also discusses the relevant research findings, clinical techniques such as imagery rescripting, and the transdiagnostic implications of Schema Therapy in addressing persistent mood symptoms. Finally, recommendations for clinical practice and areas for future research are provided.

Keywords: Schema Therapy, depression, chronic depression, early maladaptive schemas, imagery rescripting

1. Introduction

1.1 Depressive disorders and maladaptive schemas

Schema Therapy is an integrative theory and treatment model designed for psychological disorders that are deeply rooted in early childhood and adolescence and are difficult to change. It combines cognitive, behavioral, interpersonal, and experiential techniques. Developed by Jeffrey Young [1] for patients who do not benefit sufficiently from traditional Cognitive Behavioral Therapy (CBT), Schema Therapy places greater emphasis on the therapeutic relationship, emotional experience, childhood experiences and developmental processes, coping styles, and significant life events [2].

1.2 How do schemas develop?

The primary cause of early maladaptive schemas is childhood experiences. These schemas often emerge within the family context and are particularly severe when developed during early childhood. When triggered in adulthood, the emotional reactions and behaviors are often rooted in unresolved dynamics experienced with parents or family members during childhood [1, 3, 4].

 IntechOpen

There are four types of early life experiences that contribute to the formation of schemas:

1. *Frustration of needs and deprivation*

   The child is deprived of essential emotional nurturance. They may not receive sufficient empathy, love, or consistency from their environment. This experience may lead to schemas such as *Emotional Deprivation* or *Abandonment*.

2. *Traumatization or victimization*

   The child experiences abuse, neglect, or trauma. These experiences contribute to schemas such as *Mistrust/Abuse*, *Defectiveness/Shame*, and *Vulnerability to Harm or Illness*.

3. *Overindulgence of positive experiences*

   Parents may over-fulfill the child's needs, which can hinder the development of autonomy. As a result, the child may grow up without a strong sense of independence or, conversely, with an exaggerated sense of autonomy. This can lead to schemas such as *Dependence/Incompetence* or *Entitlement/Grandiosity*.

4. *Selective internalization or identification with significant others*

   The child may selectively internalize the thoughts, behaviors, or emotional patterns of important caregivers, identifying with them to varying degrees. These processes are influenced by the child's temperament and contribute to the development of specific schemas and coping styles.

2. Factors beyond childhood environment in schema formation

Factors outside of the childhood environment also play a significant role in schema development. One of the most influential factors is the child's emotional temperament. Temperament refers to the innate, unique personality traits with which an individual is born. Examples include: Sensitive—Unresponsive; Pessimistic—Optimistic; Anxious—Calm; Obsessive—Distractible; Passive—Aggressive; Irritable—Cheerful; Shy—Outgoing, and so forth.

Emotional temperament shapes how early adverse experiences influence schema formation. Different temperaments may lead to different life experiences. For example, two children who are not accepted by their parents may develop very different outcomes. One child, who is shy and emotionally dependent, might develop schemas related to *Disconnection/Rejection*, while the other, who is outgoing and socially competent, may build more adaptive schemas.

The Schema Therapy model conceptualizes psychopathology using four interrelated constructs: *core emotional needs*, *schemas*, *schema coping*, and *modes*. It is assumed that every child has basic developmental needs (e.g., the need for play, love, and attachment). When these needs are unmet—especially in interaction with inherited temperament and early environmental factors—maladaptive schemas emerge. These schemas reflect enduring beliefs and patterns about the self, others, and the world.

DOI: http://dx.doi.org/10.5772/intechopen.1011621

Schemas are not typically in conscious awareness and are made up of childhood memories, emotions, bodily sensations, and cognitions. How individuals cope with these schemas, and how schemas manifest in interpersonal patterns, gives rise to what are known as schema coping styles. These coping styles function similar to defense mechanisms in psychodynamic theory [5]. The concept of modes refers to the intense cognitive, emotional, and behavioral states that arise when multiple schemas are triggered simultaneously [6].

3. Core emotional needs

Schemas are formed when core emotional needs are not adequately met in childhood. According to Schema Therapy, there are five universal core emotional needs for all human beings:

- *Secure attachment* (safety, stability, nurturance, and acceptance)
- *Autonomy, competence, and a sense of identity*
- *Freedom to express valid needs and emotions*
- *Spontaneity and play*
- *Realistic limits and self-control*

These needs are universal and fundamental. When they are adequately met, the individual is likely to develop into a psychologically healthy adult [1].

4. Schema domains and unmet needs

According to Schema Therapy, schemas are enduring cognitive and emotional patterns that develop when core psychological needs are unmet during early life experiences. In the Turkish adaptation of the schema model, Alp Karaosmanoğlu grouped schemas under four main domains, each reflecting a cluster of unmet emotional needs: esteem, comfort/freedom, justice/security, and love [2].

- *Esteem domain:*

This domain relates to how individuals perceive their self-worth and competence. Disruptions in this area often lead to schemas such as dependence/incompetence, failure, subjugation, enmeshment, and abandonment. People with these schemas may struggle with decision-making, feel overly reliant on others, or suffer from chronic feelings of worthlessness.

- *Comfort and freedom domain:*

This domain involves regulating internal impulses, the pursuit of ease, and the need for external approval. Schemas such as approval-seeking, entitlement/grandiosity, and insufficient self-discipline/self-control belong to this group. Individuals with these schemas may show resistance to rules, act hedonistically, or constantly seek admiration and praise.

- *Justice and security domain:*

This domain pertains to the individual's sense of safety in the world and expectations of fair treatment. It includes schemas such as vulnerability to harm, negativity/pessimism, abandonment, unrelenting standards, punitiveness, self-sacrifice, and mistrust/abuse. These schemas often result in heightened threat perception, excessive responsibility, harsh self-criticism or judgment of others, and pervasive distrust in relationships.

- *Love domain:*

The love domain encompasses core emotional needs such as unconditional acceptance, belonging, and emotional sharing. Schemas that arise in this domain include emotional deprivation, social isolation, emotional inhibition, and defectiveness/shame. Individuals with impairments in this domain may struggle with forming emotional connections, expressing their feelings, or may believe they are fundamentally unlovable or unworthy of affection.

Such individuals often avoid intimacy, suppress their emotions, or feel like outsiders. These patterns contribute to deep emotional loneliness and relational difficulties, which are central concerns in psychotherapy.

5. Overview of the 18 early maladaptive schemas

Across the four domains described by Alp Karaosmanoğlu esteem, comfort/freedom, justice/security, and love—the following 18 early maladaptive schemas are identified as key targets for therapeutic intervention [2]:

1. *Emotional Deprivation*

2. *Social Isolation/Alienation*

3. *Emotional Inhibition*

4. *Defectiveness/Shame*

5. *Dependence/Incompetence*

6. *Failure*

7. *Subjugation*

8. *Enmeshment/Undeveloped Self*

9. *Abandonment/Instability*

10. *Approval-Seeking/Recognition-Seeking*

11. *Entitlement/Grandiosity*

12. *Unrelenting Standards/Hypercriticalness*

13. *Insufficient Self-Control/Self-Discipline*

14. *Punitiveness*

15. *Self-Sacrifice*

16. *Vulnerability to Harm or Illness*

17. *Negativity/Pessimism*

18. *Mistrust/Abuse*

These schemas are pervasive cognitive-affective patterns that influence an individual's perceptions, emotions, and behaviors. Because they operate largely outside of conscious awareness and are rooted in early experiences, they often become central themes to be addressed in psychotherapy.

6. Coping responses in schema therapy

People often develop specific attitudes and behavioral patterns—known as coping responses—to emotionally manage adverse life experiences. When core emotional needs are unmet during childhood and intense emotional states emerge as a result, children develop survival-driven coping strategies. Although these responses may be adaptive and protective in childhood, they often become rigid and persist into adulthood, continuing to perpetuate maladaptive schemas even when the original environmental conditions have changed [1].

Even individuals with the same schema may exhibit different coping responses to similar situations. This is because the emotional reaction is not directly dictated by the schema itself, but rather by the person's preferred coping style. In essence, while schemas shape perception and emotional reactivity, it is the coping response that determines behavior. These responses are typically automatic, habitual, and shaped by past experiences.

Rafaeli et al. explain that although coping responses may offer short-term emotional relief or a sense of safety, in the long term, they reinforce the schema and sustain the individual's psychological difficulties [7]. Over time, people tend to behave in ways that confirm and maintain their schemas, leading to a decline in life satisfaction and impaired overall functioning.

7. Coping styles in schema therapy: Surrender, avoidance, and overcompensation

In Schema Therapy, individuals use three primary coping styles to manage the emotional distress caused by activated schemas: surrender, avoidance, and overcompensation [1].

7.1 Schema surrender

In this mode, the individual passively accepts the schema as true and behaves in ways that confirm and perpetuate it. They do not attempt to resist, escape, or challenge the schema but instead adapt to it, often unconsciously reinforcing it. This leads to what is known as a *self-fulfilling prophecy*, where the individual chooses environments and people that maintain or trigger the schema. For example, someone with an *emotional deprivation schema* may repeatedly choose emotionally distant partners, thus re-experiencing unmet emotional needs and confirming the schema.

7.2 Schema avoidance

In schema avoidance, individuals behave as if the schema does not exist. They avoid situations, thoughts, emotions, or bodily sensations that might activate it. The aim is to escape discomfort or psychological pain associated with the schema. A person may show avoidance by having low expectations of themselves, avoiding challenges or responsibilities, or withdrawing emotionally. For instance, someone with a defectiveness/shame schema may believe they are unattractive and avoid looking in the mirror, thus evading the painful emotion rather than addressing it [8].

7.3 Schema overcompensation

This coping style involves behaving in the opposite way of what the schema dictates, as if doing so will nullify or "correct" the schema. These individuals may adopt aggressive, dominant, or highly confident personas to counteract deeply held feelings of inadequacy or worthlessness. Common behaviors include manipulation, power-seeking, perfectionism, or passive-aggressiveness. From the outside, such individuals may appear confident, assertive, or even grandiose, but internally, they are still driven by the unmet needs and emotional pain of the schema. For example, someone with a *subjugation schema* may become highly defiant and oppositional to avoid ever feeling controlled again.

8. Temperament, early experiences, and schema activation

The functioning of the nervous system—and its patterns of emotional and behavioral responses—is shaped by an interplay of *temperament, genetic predispositions*, and *early life experiences*.

9. Schema Therapy: An integrative approach to restructuring early maladaptive schemas

Schema Therapy is a comprehensive psychotherapeutic model that focuses primarily on childhood origins of *early maladaptive schemas (EMSs)*. The core aim of the therapy is to restructure these persistent and dysfunctional patterns that develop when core emotional needs are unmet during early development.

Two primary techniques form the foundation of Schema Therapy:

- *Limited reparenting:*

This involves the therapist meeting the client's unmet emotional needs within appropriate therapeutic boundaries. Through a corrective emotional experience, the therapist provides a reparative relationship that fosters trust, validation, and emotional security.

- *Imagery rescripting:*

This technique involves guided visualization in which past emotionally charged experiences are revisited and transformed. The client reimagines these events in ways that meet their core emotional needs, allowing for emotional healing and cognitive reprocessing.

Together, these techniques allow clients to reinterpret past schema-driven experiences and to develop healthier emotional and behavioral coping mechanisms.

10. Transdiagnostic relevance of early maladaptive schemas

Early maladaptive schemas are not exclusive to personality disorders. They are increasingly recognized as playing a significant role in a wide range of clinical conditions, including:

- *Depression*
- *Anxiety disorders*
- *Post-traumatic stress disorder (PTSD)*
- *Eating disorders*
- *Psychotic disorders*
- *Substance use disorders*
- *Obsessive-compulsive disorder (OCD)*

In these disorders, EMSs are often linked to persistent cognitive-behavioral patterns and interpersonal dysfunctions. Research suggests that schemas contribute not only to the onset of these disorders but also to their chronicity and resistance to treatment.

Therefore, schemas offer a *transdiagnostic framework* that is both clinically meaningful and therapeutically actionable. They can serve as core treatment targets across various psychiatric diagnoses, enhancing both assessment and intervention strategies.

11. Early maladaptive schemas in depressive disorders

According to Aaron Beck, negative schemas develop as a result of adverse life events, often beginning in childhood [9]. In individuals with depression, these schemas are reinforced through cognitive distortions—systematic errors in thinking that maintain and strengthen negative beliefs. When a stressful or adverse event occurs, these dormant schemas are activated, leading the individual to interpret experiences in a pessimistic and distorted manner.

In depression, individuals tend to modify their perception of events to fit their pre-existing maladaptive schemas, rather than interpreting situations objectively. Because they cannot exert cognitive control over these thought patterns, they process reality through the lens of distorted schemas, which exacerbates their depressive symptoms.

For example, an individual exposed to *emotional neglect, abuse, or inconsistent parenting* during childhood may develop an *abandonment schema*. In adulthood, triggering events such as the end of a romantic relationship or the loss of a loved one can activate this schema, resulting in overwhelming depressive affect.

Depressed individuals often fluctuate between avoidance of negative emotions and surrendering to them, rather than addressing them adaptively. This schema-driven coping reinforces the depressive state [10].

Similarly, a person who develops a *failure schema* due to repeated criticism, unrealistic expectations, or lack of support during childhood may become particularly vulnerable to depressive symptoms when faced with challenges like job loss, academic failure, or financial hardship in adulthood. Instead of adapting constructively, the individual may engage in dysfunctional coping mechanisms that further reinforce the belief of inadequacy, perpetuating the depressive cycle.

These examples highlight how early maladaptive schemas act as vulnerability factors in depression, contributing to both the *onset* and *maintenance* of the disorder, as well as complicating the therapeutic process if left unaddressed.

12. Maladaptive schemas commonly associated with depression

A growing body of research has demonstrated strong links between early maladaptive schemas (EMSs) and the development, severity, and persistence of depressive disorders. Key findings in the literature include the following:

- Defectiveness/Shame, Insufficient Self-Control, and Self-Sacrifice schemas are found to be significantly more prevalent among individuals diagnosed with depression [11]

- Cognitive characteristics are shown to mediate the relationship between parenting styles and symptoms of anxiety and depression. That is, how individuals interpret and internalize early parental interactions plays a critical role in their vulnerability to mood disorders [11, 12]

- The Failure, Emotional Deprivation, and Abandonment/Instability schemas are consistently observed at higher rates in depressed individuals compared to healthy controls [10]

DOI: http://dx.doi.org/10.5772/intechopen.1011621

- Emotional Deprivation and Social Isolation schemas have been identified as mediators in the relationship between childhood physical/emotional abuse and adult depression [13]

- The severity of depressive symptoms is significantly associated with elevations in two schema domains:

    o *Disconnection and Rejection*

    o Impaired Autonomy and Performance [14]

- Compared to control groups, individuals with a diagnosis of depression show elevations across all schema domains, supporting the transdiagnostic relevance of EMSs in depressive disorders [15, 16]

- Specific schemas Dependence/Incompetence, Defectiveness/Shame, Abandonment/Instability, Mistrust/Abuse, and Social Isolation—have been strongly correlated with depression severity [17, 18]

These findings highlight the significant role of EMSs in the cognitive-emotional architecture of depression. Schema-focused interventions may therefore offer promising targets for both symptom reduction and relapse prevention in depressive disorders.

This systematic review conducted by Taylor et al. examined the effectiveness of Schema Therapy in reducing early maladaptive schemas and psychiatric symptoms [19]. Out of 1563 studies reviewed, only 12 were deemed methodologically adequate and included in the analysis. Most of these studies reported significant improvements both in schema levels and in clinical symptoms. For instance, in a case series conducted by Malogiannis et al., mode-based schema therapy was found to be effective in individuals diagnosed with chronic depression [20]. However, more controlled studies are needed to enhance the generalizability of the findings. While promising results have been observed, particularly in personality disorders, the evidence remains limited for other psychiatric diagnoses [21].

The study conducted by Ahmadpanah et al. investigated whether a history of suicide attempts in individuals diagnosed with major depression is associated with specific early maladaptive schemas [22]. The findings revealed that the schemas of emotional deprivation, social isolation, shame, and abandonment were significantly associated with a history of suicide attempts. These results suggest that examining schema-level features in clinical assessments, particularly in cases of depression, may offer important insights into suicide risk.

The systematic review and meta-analysis conducted by Bishop et al. aimed to comprehensively evaluate findings on the relationship between early maladaptive schemas (EMSs) and depression [23]. According to the meta-analytic results, all EMSs were found to be significantly positively associated with depression. In particular, the schemas of social isolation and defectiveness/shame showed strong associations with depressive symptoms. The findings suggest that individuals who feel unworthy, inadequate, or unlovable tend to report higher levels of depressive symptoms. However, as the majority of the studies included were cross-sectional in design, causal relationships could not be clearly established. The researchers recommend the development of preventive and therapeutic interventions that specifically target themes of social isolation and defectiveness.

The systematic review conducted by Bär et al. examined the presence and patterns of EMSs and schema modes across various clinical disorders [24]. While Schema Therapy is most commonly applied in the treatment of personality disorders, this review systematically assessed the extent to which EMSs and schema modes are present in different diagnostic groups. The findings indicate that, although evidence for EMSs is limited in some disorders, meaningful patterns emerge across a wide range of clinical conditions. The authors highlight that EMSs may represent a transdiagnostic vulnerability framework, and the associated schema modes could serve as functional targets for clinical intervention.

This review highlights that numerous studies conducted across different countries have found individuals with major depressive disorder (MDD) to exhibit significant differences in EMSs. For instance, Ahmadpanah et al. reported that individuals with MDD had significantly higher levels of schemas such as social isolation, defectiveness, abandonment, punitiveness, and dependence compared to both clinical and healthy control groups [22]. Similarly, Flink et al. found that individuals with MDD scored higher than controls on schemas of social isolation, negativity/pessimism, defectiveness, and emotional deprivation [25]. In line with these findings, Halvorsen et al. reported that the schemas of defectiveness, emotional deprivation, and enmeshment were more pronounced in the MDD group [26]. A study by Özdel et al. also found that individuals with MDD exhibited significantly higher levels of schemas such as defectiveness, social isolation, punitiveness, dependence, and insufficient self-control compared to other groups [27]. Wang et al. reported that individuals with MDD scored higher on schemas such as social isolation, defectiveness, emotional inhibition, and abandonment when compared to both clinical and non-clinical samples [28]. In another study, Darvoodi et al. found that the MDD group differed significantly from the control group in the schemas of social isolation, defectiveness, and self-sacrifice [29].

These findings suggest that major depression is associated not only with negative automatic thoughts at the cognitive level, but also with more deeply rooted schematic structures. In particular, schemas such as *social isolation*, *defectiveness*, and *abandonment* appear to be commonly observed in individuals experiencing depression.

In conclusion, individuals with depressive disorders tend to score high on nearly all early maladaptive schemas (EMSs), with the exception of the *entitlement/grandiosity* schema, which was found to be elevated in only about half of the studies. Among all schemas, *emotional deprivation* and *social isolation* have been identified as particularly prominent in depression.

One of the most challenging clinical situations in treatment is chronic depression, for which the existing literature is more limited. A single-case series study conducted by Malogiannis et al. aimed to evaluate the effectiveness of Schema Therapy (ST) in individuals diagnosed with chronic depression [20]. A total of 12 patients received an individualized treatment protocol consisting of 60 sessions. The intervention followed an A–B–C design: an initial waiting period (A), followed by the establishment of therapeutic alliance and engagement (B), and finally, intensive schema-focused intervention (C).

At the end of treatment, approximately 60% of participants either achieved remission or showed marked clinical improvement. Hamilton Depression Rating Scale scores significantly decreased, and these improvements were largely maintained at a 6-month follow-up.

The study suggests that Schema Therapy may be a promising approach in the treatment of chronic depression. However, the absence of a control group and the small sample size limit the generalizability of the findings.

When an individual experiences intense shame, their sense of belonging can be damaged, leading to feelings of loneliness and disconnection. Considering the fundamental human need to feel accepted and welcomed within a community or group [30] the early maladaptive schemas of social isolation and defectiveness/shame may hinder the process of connection and belonging, thereby increasing the risk for mood disorders and other mental health conditions.

Family problems, an anxious temperament in childhood, and low self-esteem in early adulthood have been associated with chronic depression [31]. Childhood maltreatment has been shown to increase the risk of developing chronic depression and is associated with poorer treatment response [32]. A close relationship between chronic depression and Axis II personality disorders has also been emphasized [33]. Among individuals with dysthymia, personality disorder rates can be as high as 65% [34]. In patients with chronic depression, Cluster C personality traits have predicted poorer outcomes.

A schema-based model proposed for chronic depression explains the interaction between distal factors—such as early adverse life experiences and personality pathology—and early maladaptive schemas (EMSs), which are triggered by life events (e.g., loss and failure) and maintained by avoidance-based coping strategies [35]. Psychotherapeutic interventions that are longer in duration and more intensive, targeting underlying psychological factors like childhood trauma and maladaptive schemas, may yield more effective outcomes in the treatment of chronic depression.

A multiple single-case series study by Renner et al. (2016) aimed to assess the effectiveness of individual Schema Therapy (ST) in patients diagnosed with chronic major depression. Twenty-five participants first underwent a baseline observation period without treatment lasting 6–24 weeks, followed by a 12-week exploration phase to assess their schema-related patterns. This was followed by an average of 65 individual ST sessions. The findings demonstrated significant and robust reductions in depression symptoms as measured by the Beck Depression Inventory-II (BDI-II) and the Quick Inventory of Depressive Symptomatology (QIDS). These results indicate that Schema Therapy is an effective intervention for reducing chronic depressive symptoms [36].

Chronic depression is often rooted in traumatic childhood experiences and personality pathology [37, 38]. Today, short-term and symptom-focused treatments may be insufficient to adequately address these underlying factors. Schema therapy (ST), as a psychological treatment with a strong focus on childhood experiences and personality pathology, has been proposed as an effective approach for chronic depression [35].

Schema Therapy has already demonstrated its efficacy in treating borderline personality disorder and, notably, Cluster C personality disorders [39]. Brewin et al. reported that imagery rescripting, one of the core techniques of ST, had substantial and positive effects on depressive symptoms in individuals with chronic depression [40].

In a randomized controlled trial (RCT), Carter et al. compared a brief ST protocol with cognitive therapy (CT) and found comparable remission rates. While these early findings are promising, the effects of ST on chronic depression need to be further evaluated in studies involving a sufficient number of sessions [41].

Building on previous work, the present study tested the effectiveness of up to 65 individual ST sessions in 25 patients with chronic depression using a multiple baseline single-case series design. Single-case series are important research designs in the development of new treatments. They are considered alternatives to cohort and case-control studies and typically require smaller sample sizes than RCTs. The strength of the multiple-baseline design used in this study—unlike the single-baseline case series by Malogiannis et al. [20]—is that it allows attribution of symptom improvement to the intervention itself rather than to the mere passage of time, in a manner comparable to RCTs.

Another advantage of this study is the inclusion of an exploration phase, during which therapists were instructed not to intervene to alter symptoms, apart from the randomly determined baseline period. We hypothesized that Schema Therapy would lead to a reduction in depressive symptom severity compared to both the untreated control (baseline) phase and the exploration phase.

The findings of the present study also offer potential insights into the mechanisms of change in Schema Therapy (ST) for chronic depression. In psychotherapy research, the question of what drives symptom change—namely, treatment mechanisms—has been a subject of ongoing debate. Some researchers argue that improvements in symptoms are due to treatment-specific factors, while others contend that common factors, such as the therapeutic alliance (especially in the early phase), are primarily responsible for symptom change.

The exploratory phase in the current study included elements typically regarded as common factors, such as the establishment of a strong therapeutic relationship. However, symptom improvement was not associated with this exploratory phase but rather occurred during the intervention phase. This suggests that common factors alone may not sufficiently explain symptom change in ST and that the specific techniques introduced in the intervention phase are likely critical for producing clinical improvement. Nevertheless, this study did not directly test mechanisms of change, and further research is needed to better understand how change occurs in Schema Therapy for chronic depression.

Another important issue frequently encountered in chronic depression is childhood traumatic experiences. One study examined the relationship between childhood trauma and the chronicity of depression using a large and representative sample [37]. The findings revealed that childhood trauma was significantly associated with depressive episodes lasting 24 months or longer. Notably, individuals with higher cumulative index scores—calculated based on the frequency of childhood trauma—had a markedly increased likelihood of developing chronic depression. Even after controlling for variables such as anxiety disorders, depression severity, and age of onset, the relationship between childhood trauma and chronic depression remained statistically significant. These findings suggest that childhood trauma may be an independent determinant contributing to the persistent nature of depression.

In Schema Therapy, the primary aim of treatment is to help clients meet their core emotional needs by modifying their maladaptive schemas, coping responses, and schema modes within the context of adaptive behaviors. The difficulties experienced by individuals often follow a persistent and long-standing course, which limits the effectiveness of traditional therapeutic approaches. In particular, poor treatment response or the recurrent nature of these disorders often points to the presence of deeper, underlying structural problems.

In some cases, a specific diagnosis may not be clearly established; however, the psychological difficulties faced by the individual may present with a chronic and pervasive character. These individuals frequently exhibit long-term, dysfunctional interpersonal relationship patterns. Moreover, excessive avoidance behaviors, rigid and inflexible thought patterns, and behavioral styles are commonly observed. Some individuals may also display excessive dependency, persistent clinging, or, at times, grandiose attitudes.

This clinical picture highlights the importance of assessing and addressing underlying personality structures. Schema Therapy becomes especially relevant in such cases, offering a structured framework to target and modify entrenched patterns that are not adequately addressed by conventional therapeutic methods.

13. Treatment

The classic protocol for imagery rescripting (ImRs) consists of three phases. In the first phase, the patient is invited to focus on a distressing memory that carries an emotional tone similar to their current symptomatology. Ideally, this memory should stem from a childhood event. At this stage, the therapist encourages the patient to speak in the present tense from the perspective of the child [42].

Once factual details are clarified, the therapist inquiries about the child's emotions and unmet needs. The second phase begins with the rescripting process, during which the patient, as their adult self, attempts to understand, protect, and care for the child version of themselves. This may involve preventing the mistreatment, creating a safe environment, or doing anything the patient considers appropriate to meet the child's needs.

In the third phase, the child may request further support from the adult self, and the intervention continues until these needs are fully addressed.

In this context, imagery rescripting serves as a powerful tool not only for modifying traumatic memories but also for emotionally redefining the self. A change in self-representation may help explain the transdiagnostic efficacy of ImRs. ImRs reduced the development of intrusive memories, in part by diminishing guilt-related cognitions [42, 43].

Despite the well-established efficacy of cognitive therapy for depression, a significant proportion of individuals still show limited treatment response. Treatment-resistant residual symptoms remain a challenge with an estimated 40% of patients failing to respond even to initial treatments [44]. This highlights the pressing need to enhance treatment efficacy and broaden available therapeutic options.

To address this challenge, several key considerations have emerged:

- *Understanding heterogeneity beyond diagnostic categories* is essential for improving treatment outcomes. A more nuanced approach can help tailor interventions to individual profiles.

- *Intrusive mental imagery* has gained attention as a transdiagnostic feature that plays a role in both the pathogenesis and treatment of depression. These involuntary and vivid sensory intrusions—often tied to negative past experiences—are frequently observed in individuals with depression and are thought to contribute to the severity and chronicity of the disorder.

- Experimental studies have demonstrated that imagery has a stronger emotional impact than verbal processing, for both negative and positive emotions. In Schema Therapy, one of the core techniques—imagery rescripting (ImRs)—uses guided imagination to modify distressing autobiographical memories. By mentally reworking these past experiences, ImRs helps transform threatening memories into more benign or supportive narratives [45].

These insights underscore the potential of imagery-based interventions to address depressive symptoms, especially in treatment-resistant cases [46].

14. Conclusion

Schema Therapy provides a comprehensive and effective framework for addressing chronic depression, particularly in cases where the disorder is rooted in early childhood trauma and co-occurring personality pathology. Personality traits and maladaptive personality structures—often shaped by adverse early experiences—play a critical role in both the onset and persistence of chronic depressive symptoms. These entrenched patterns are frequently resistant to conventional treatments and contribute to long-standing interpersonal difficulties and emotional dysregulation. By targeting EMSs dysfunctional coping styles, and maladaptive schema modes, Schema Therapy facilitates the restructuring of deeply ingrained cognitive-emotional patterns that underlie both chronic mood disturbances and maladaptive personality functioning. Techniques such as limited reparenting and imagery rescripting offer opportunities for corrective emotional experiences and schema modification, fostering greater emotional flexibility and healthier interpersonal relationships. As research continues to support the transdiagnostic relevance of EMSs across mood and personality disorders, integrating Schema Therapy into clinical practice represents a promising avenue for improving outcomes in this complex and challenging patient population. Further controlled studies are warranted to enhance the empirical basis for its use in chronic depression and to clarify the mechanisms of change involved.

Acknowledgements

The author confirms the use of ChatGPT (OpenAI) only for language editing purposes.

Author details

Ayse Dondu
Department of Psychiatry, Faculty of Medicine, Aydın Adnan Menderes University, Aydın, Turkey

*Address all correspondence to: ayse.dondu@adu.edu.tr

References

[1] Young JE, Klosko JS, Weishaar ME. Schema Therapy: A practitioner's Guide. New York: Guilford Press; 2006

[2] Karaosmanoğlu HA, Köse B, Aytaç M, et al. A new model for basic needs: Comparison of the second order factorial structures of young schema questionnaire and its relationship with symptoms of psychopathology. Current Psychology. 2024;**43**:24565-24580

[3] Martin R, Young J. Schema Therapy. Handbook of Cognitive-Behavioral Therapies. 2010. p. 317

[4] Arntz A, Rijkeboer M, Chan E, Fassbinder E, Karaosmanoglu A, Lee CW, et al. Towards a reformulated theory underlying schema therapy: Position paper of an international workgroup. Cognitive Therapy and Research. 2021:1-14

[5] Arntz A, Jacob G. Schema Therapy in Practice: An Introductory Guide to the Schema Mode Approach. Chichester: Wiley-Blackwell; 2016

[6] Farrell JM, Reiss N, Shaw IA. The Schema Therapy Clinician's Guide: A Complete Resource for Building and Delivering Individual, Group and Integrated Schema Mode Treatment Programs. Wiley-Blackwell; 2015

[7] Rafaeli E, Bernstein DP, Young J. Schema Therapy: Distinctive Features. London: Routledge; 2011

[8] Arntz A, Genderen H. Schema Therapy for Borderline Personality Disorder. 2020. Print ISBN:9781119101048, Online ISBN:9781119101161. DOI: 10.1002/9781119101161

[9] Beck AT, Rush AJ, Shaw BF, Emery G. Cognitive Therapy of Depression. New York: Guilford Press; 1979

[10] Renner F, Lobbestael J, Peeters F, Arntz A, Huibers M, Speckens A. Early maladaptive schemas in depressed patients: Stability and relation with depressive symptoms over the course of treatment. Journal of Affective Disorders. 2013;**149**(1-3):435-442

[11] McGinn LK, Cukor D, Sanderson WC. The relationship between parenting style and cognitive vulnerability to depression: The role of core beliefs. Cognitive Therapy and Research. 2005;**29**(3):295-311

[12] Shah R, Waller G. Parental style and vulnerability to depression: The role of core beliefs. Journal of Nervous and Mental Disease. 2000;**188**(1):19-25

[13] Lumley MN, Harkness KL. Specificity in the relations among childhood adversity, early maladaptive schemas, and symptom profiles in adolescent depression. Cognitive Therapy and Research. 2007;**31**(5):639-657

[14] Konukçu HB, Akkoyunlu S, Türkçapar MH. Early maladaptive schemas in depressed women and its relationship with depression. Journal of Cognitive Behavioral Psychotherapies and Research. 2013;**2**(2):98-105

[15] Riso LP, du Toit PL, Blandino JA, Penna S, Dacey S, et al. Cognitive aspects of chronic depression. In: Riso LP et al., editors. Cognitive Schemas and Core Beliefs in Psychological Problems: A Scientist–Practitioner Guide. Washington, DC: American Psychological Association; 2003. pp. 51-75

[16] Lapsekili N, Ak M. Bipolar ve unipolar depresyonda erken dönem uyumsuz şemalar: Benzerlikler

ve farklılıklar. Bilişsel Davranışçı Psikoterapi ve Araştırmalar Dergisi. 2012;**1**(3):145-151

[17] Schmidt NB, Joiner TE, Young JE, Telch MJ. The schema questionnaire: Investigation of psychometric properties and the hierarchical structure of a measure of maladaptive schemas. Cognitive Therapy and Research. 1995;**19**(3):295-321

[18] Harris AE, Curtin L. Parental perceptions, early maladaptive schemas, and depressive symptoms in young adults. Cognitive Therapy and Research. 2002;**26**(3):405-416

[19] Taylor CDJ, Bee P, Haddock G. Does schema therapy change schemas and symptoms? A systematic review across mental health disorders. Psychology and Psychotherapy: Theory, Research and Practice. 2017;**90**(3):456-479

[20] Malogiannis IA, Arntz A, Spyropoulou A, Tsartsara E, Aggeli A, Karveli S, et al. Schema therapy for patients with chronic depression: A single case series study. Journal of Behavior Therapy and Experimental Psychiatry. 2014;**45**(3):319-327

[21] Jacob GA, Arntz A. Schema therapy for personality disorders—A review. International Journal of Cognitive Therapy. 2013;**6**(2):171-185. DOI: 10.1521/ijct.2013.6.2.171

[22] Ahmadpanah M, Astinsadaf S, Akhondi A, Haghighi M, Sadeghi Bahmani D, Nazaribadie M, et al. Early maladaptive schemas of emotional deprivation, social isolation, shame and abandonment are related to a history of suicide attempts among patients with major depressive disorders. Comprehensive Psychiatry. 2017;**77**:79

[23] Bishop A, Younan R, Low J, Pilkington PD. Early maladaptive schemas and depression in adulthood: A systematic review and meta-analysis. Clinical Psychology and Psychotherapy. 2021;**28**(6):1524-1538

[24] Bär A, Bär HE, Rijkeboer MM, Lobbestael J. Early maladaptive schemas and schema modes in clinical disorders: A systematic review. Psychology and Psychotherapy: Theory, Research and Practice. 2023;**96**(3):657-676

[25] Flink N, Honkalampi K, Lehto SM, Leppänen V, Viinamäki H, Lindeman S. Comparison of early maladaptive schemas between borderline personality disorder and chronic depression. Clinical Psychology & Psychotherapy. 2018;**25**(4):532-539. DOI: 10.1002/cpp.2188

[26] Halvorsen MS, Wang CEA, Eisemann M, Waterloo K. Early maladaptive schemas, temperament and character traits in clinically depressed and previously depressed subjects. Clinical Psychology & Psychotherapy. 2009;**16**(5):394-407

[27] Özdel K, İlhan İÖ. Personality disorders and depression. Turkiye Klinikleri Journal of Internal Medical Sciences. 2007;**3**(12):82-86

[28] Wang CE, Halvorsen M, Eisemann M. Stability of dysfunctional attitudes and early maladaptive schemas: A 9-year follow-up study of clinically depressed subjects. Journal of Behavior Therapy and Experimental Psychiatry. 2010;**41**(4):389-396

[29] Davoodi E, Wen A, Dobson KS, Noorbala AA, Mohammadi A, Farahmand Z. Early maladaptive schemas in depression and somatization disorder. Journal of Affective Disorders. 2018;**235**:82-89. DOI: 10.1016/j.jad.2018.04.017. Epub 2018 Apr 3

[30] Schore A. Right brain-to-right brain psychotherapy: Recent scientific and

clinical advances. Annals of General Psychiatry. 2022;**21**(1):46. DOI: 10.1186/s12991-022-00420-3

[31] Angst J, Gamma A, Rössler W, Ajdacic V, Klein DN. Long-term depression versus episodic major depression: Results from the prospective Zurich study of a community sample. Journal of Affective Disorders. 2009;**115**(1-2):112-121. DOI: 10.1016/j.jad.2008.09.023. Epub 2008 Oct 29

[32] Nanni V, Uher R, Danese A. Childhood maltreatment predicts unfavorable course of illness and treatment outcome in depression: A meta-analysis. The American Journal of Psychiatry. 2012;**169**(2):141-151

[33] Maddux RE, Riso LP, Klein DN, Markowitz JC, Rothbaum BO, Arnow BA, et al. Select comorbid personality disorders and the treatment of chronic depression with nefazodone, targeted psychotherapy, or their combination. Journal of Affective Disorders. 2009;**117**(3):174-179

[34] Pepper CM, Klein DN, Anderson RL, Riso LP, Ouimette PC, Lizardi H. DSM-III-R axis II comorbidity in dysthymia and major depression. American Journal of Psychiatry. 1995;**152**(2):239-247. DOI: 10.1176/ajp.152.2.239

[35] Renner F, Arntz A, Leeuw I, Huibers MJH. Treatment for chronic depression using schema therapy. Clinical Psychology: Science and Practice. 2013;**20**(2):161-176

[36] Renner F, Arntz A, Peeters FPML, Lobbestael J, Huibers MJH. Schema therapy for chronic depression: Results of a multiple single case series. Journal of Behavior Therapy and Experimental Psychiatry. 2016;**51**:66-73

[37] Wiersma JE, Hovens JGFM, van Oppen P, Giltay EJ, van Schaik DJF, Beekman ATF, et al. The importance of childhood trauma and childhood life events for chronicity of depression in adults. Journal of Clinical Psychiatry. 2009;**70**(7):983-989

[38] Kronström K, Salminen JK, Hietala J, Kajander J, Vahlberg T, Markkula J, et al. Personality traits and recovery from major depressive disorder. Nordic Journal of Psychiatry. 2011;**65**(1):52-57. DOI: 10.3109/08039488.2010.487571. Epub 2010 May 26

[39] Bamelis LLM, Evers SMAA, Spinhoven P, Arntz A. Results of a multicenter randomized controlled trial of the clinical effectiveness of schema therapy for personality disorders. American Journal of Psychiatry. 2013;**171**(3):305-322

[40] Brewin CR, Wheatley J, Patel T, Fearon P, Hackmann A, Wells A, et al. Imagery rescripting as a brief stand-alone treatment for depressed patients with intrusive memories. Behaviour Research and Therapy. 2009;**47**(7):569-576

[41] Carter JD, McIntosh VVW, Jordan J, Porter RJ, Frampton CMA, Joyce PR. Psychotherapy for depression: A randomized clinical trial comparing schema therapy and cognitive therapy. Journal of Affective Disorders. 2013;**151**(2):500-505

[42] Mancini A, Mancini F. Rescripting memory, redefining the self: A meta-emotional perspective on the hypothesized mechanism(s) of imagery rescripting. Frontiers in Psychology. 2018;**9**:581

[43] Hagenaars MA, Arntz A. Reduced intrusion development after post-trauma imagery rescripting: An experimental study. Journal of Behavior Therapy and Experimental Psychiatry. 2012;**43**(2):808-814

[44] Hollon SD, Ponniah K. A review of empirically supported psychological therapies for mood disorders in adults. Depression and Anxiety. 2010;**27**(10):891-932

[45] Holmes EA, Arntz A, Smucker MR. Imagery rescripting in cognitive behavior therapy: Images, treatment techniques, and outcomes. Journal of Behavior Therapy and Experimental Psychiatry. 2007;**38**(4):297-305

[46] Ma OYT, Lo BCY. Is it magic? An exploratory randomized controlled trial comparing imagery rescripting and cognitive restructuring in the treatment of depression. Journal of Behavior Therapy and Experimental Psychiatry. 2022;**75**:101721